Praise for Ray Zinn and *Tough Things First*

"*Tough Things First* is not a typical business book about a market success or effective business methods. It is about the success of one Silicon Valley startup, Micrel, which has been run profitably by the same CEO/founder for 37 years. It is about how a founder's dedication to basic principles is required to make any startup successful. The precise recipe for success may change—for example, my 32-year-old company, Cypress Semiconductor, used venture funding, while Zinn preached and achieved financial independence—but Zinn shows how startups must have and truly practice their core values to succeed."

—T. J. Rodgers, President and CEO of Cypress Semiconductor Corp.

"The disciplined pursuit of what is essential is ten times harder than the undisciplined pursuit of the nonessential, but it is a hundred times more valuable. This is brilliantly illustrated in *Tough Things First*."

—Greg McKeown, author of the *New York Times* bestseller *Essentialism*

"Unlike many management books I've read, *Tough Things First* is entertaining, enlightening, humorous, as well as truly practical. It is not just for tech types. Executives and entrepreneurs from every industry, as well as those in business school, will find it relevant and insightful.

"I have known many Micrel employees, and they were there because of Ray and his approach to leadership. This book shares what made Micrel a special place and how you can live life on your terms to make your business, your vision, and your dreams a reality and a success.

"After reading this book, you may not be able to do a one-armed push-up as Ray can, but you will learn a philosophy, the importance of discipline, and practical advice to do the tough things first and become a leader, build a lasting culture, and master your industry profession."

—Mike Noonen, Chairman of Silicon Catalyst

"Ray Zinn has chronicled the discipline, the cultural foundation blocks, and the tough decisions required of a successful startup. Ray explains how discipline defines success under his four principles: focus, short time frames, frugality, and being the best."

—Michael Shepherd, President and CEO of Bank of the West

"At a time when a rush-to-riches attitude prevails in Silicon Valley, it's refreshing to get a dose of perspective from a veteran. Ray Zinn reminds us all that conviction, discipline, and perspective are still keys to success—not lucky timing with an app. *Tough Things First* is Ray Zinn's manifesto for entrepreneurs. It is a must-read for anyone interested in a successful career."

—Richard A. Moran, PhD, President of Menlo College and author of *Sins and CEOs*

"Ray Zinn's journey is not only a genuine Silicon Valley success story but also a remarkable life story from which nearly anyone can draw important lessons. In *Tough Things First*, Ray explores not only the how-to aspects of building a company but also the mindset and character traits— discipline, intense focus, and attention to detail—needed for lasting entrepreneurial success. Most important, in an era when success is too often defined by publicity, speedy exits, and financial windfalls, Ray reminds us that the fulfillment of building a thriving, enduring enterprise is the reward that a true entrepreneur seeks."

—Balu Balakrishnan, CEO of Power Integrations

"Wow! *Tough Things First* is a read that you won't want to miss. From beginning to end, this book shares tough lessons every entrepreneur needs to know. Along with his incredible personal drive, which helped propel him to success, Zinn points out the tough lessons he learned early and how you can use those same lessons. Executives and entrepreneurs will find this book compelling.

"Ray Zinn is not the kind of man you want to tell that something can't be done. He shows it can—and how he did it. He learned the tough things first, and now he is sharing those tough things with us. What a philosophy!"

—Dr. Richard G. Whitehead, university ambassador of Southern Virginia University

"Covering Micrel as a sell-side analyst was a real pleasure for me personally. It wasn't so much because the company represented one of the hot stocks—it certainly did—but because the man at the helm was Ray Zinn. Here's this very dynamic, very unique individual who at the time was still running the company that he had founded 20 years prior. Impressively, Ray would go on to run Micrel for nearly 20 more years, and that's no small feat when you consider how highly competitive and notoriously cyclical the chip industry is.

"Outside of tremendous stamina, I think the first thing that jumps to mind when I think about Ray is his great integrity as a manager and as a person: honesty, fairness, the way he treats everyone around him and expects to be treated. Ray is also one of the more effective communicators I've known. He is very much a straight shooter, very transparent in his dealings with people, and very direct. With reason, there are no hidden agendas. What you see is what you get. Ray is also extremely generous with his time. I think that comes from a genuine respect he has for people. If you're going to spend a good part of your day focused on issues important to him or his company, then he's going to reciprocate by giving his undivided attention to you. If you are lucky enough to spend some time with Ray and you keep your ears open, you will pick up pearls of wisdom along the way. At his core, I believe Ray Zinn is a teacher. For me, that has definitely been a good thing."

—Douglas Lee, CEO of Marinwood Capital Management

"The one thing that always struck me about Ray Zinn was his sincere belief that a company's most significant valuable asset was its people and his unrelenting focus on trying to make each and every one of us a better person—whether it was to make you more patient, more tolerant, or more temperate. The fact that Micrel was started with a fairly limited amount of financing is probably one of the keys to the value that he built at the company. Essentially, Ray increased the value of the company by increasing the value of its employees."

—Jung-Chen Lin, VP of LAN Solutions at Micrel

"Ray believes that an enduring company should have a simple but strong culture. The four pillars that Ray fostered in Micrel are honesty, integrity, the dignity of every individual, and doing whatever it takes. This corporate culture is the guiding principal that we've followed in our daily work. Culture is passed along by communication and imitation from one generation to the next. However, a company consists of people from different backgrounds. Communicating culture can be a challenge. Ray took every possible opportunity to give talks or ask the staff to speak every Friday. He believed that good employees make good companies.

—Wiren Perera, VP of LAN Solutions and Corporate Strategic Marketing at Micrel

TOUGH
THINGS
FIRST

TOUGH
THINGS
FIRST

Leadership Lessons from Silicon Valley's
Longest-Serving CEO

RAY ZINN

NEW YORK   CHICAGO   SAN FRANCISCO

ATHENS   LONDON   MADRID   MEXICO CITY

MILAN   NEW DELHI   SINGAPORE

SYDNEY   TORONTO

Copyright © 2016 by McGraw-Hill Education. All rights reserved. Printed in the United States of America. Except as permitted under the United States Copyright Act of 1976, no part of this publication may be reproduced or distributed in any form or by any means, or stored in a data base or retrieval system, without prior written permission of the publisher.

1 2 3 4 5 6 7 8 9 0   DOC/DOC   1 2 1 0 9 8 7 6 5

ISBN: 978-1-259-58417-6
MHID: 1-259-58417-8

e-ISBN: 978-1-259-58418-3
e-MHID: 1-259-58418-6

Library of Congress Cataloging-in-Publication Data

Zinn, Ray.
  Tough things first : leadership lessons from Silicon Valley's longest serving CEO / Ray Zinn.
    pages cm
  ISBN 978-1-259-58417-6 — ISBN 1-259-58417-8 (alk. paper) 1. Leadership. 2. Corporate culture. 3. Entrepreneurship. I. Title.
  HD57.7Z557 2016

                                                    658.4'092—dc23

McGraw-Hill Education books are available at special quantity discounts to use as premiums and sales promotions, or for use in corporate training programs. To contact a representative, please visit the Contact Us page at www.mhprofessional.com.

To my life partner, DeLona, the most wonderful wife a man could have, whose undying support allowed me to push through 37 years with Micrel, through the trauma of going blind, and yet always enjoying each day.

And to Warren H. Muller, my partner and Micrel's cofounder, who I have missed every day since he passed in 2008. Without Warren, Micrel might never have gotten off the ground.

CONTENTS

PART II

ENTREPRENEURIALISM: BUILDING COMPANIES THAT LAST THROUGH THE AGES

PREFACE

Running the high hurdles isn't easy when you are vertically challenged.

Yet despite being only 5 feet, 8 inches (173 cm)—markedly shorter than the other boys in starting blocks on my high school's running track—I was about to sprint past them, bounding over 42-inch (107 cm) hurdles and finishing first. This came as a surprise to our track and field coach, who a few months earlier had said to me, "You're too short. This is not something that somebody your size should be doing."

My friends and I were track and field runners who decided to jump a few hurdles for fun. Hurdling was not our sport, and we inexpertly knocked most of the barricades down. I managed to topple all of them, snapping one on impact. The coach was sensibly upset with me for breaking the gear his hurdle runners needed, but his words stung for other reasons. I wasn't sore that he tried to embarrass me in front of my friends and the other track athletes despite the fact that I was a little sensitive about my height.

What bothered me was his assumption that I could not do something.

My father—an Imperial Valley rancher keenly aware of changes in the environment—noticed that I was oddly quiet that evening. He folded his evening newspaper, got up from his favorite chair, and asked what might be troubling me. I gave him the whole story, and with only a short pause afterward he asked, "What are you going to do?"

The answer was already on my lips: "I'd like to learn to run the hurdles." I knew it would require a lot of learning. Striding over hurdles depends on technique learned through days and months of repetitive practice. For me it would be tougher still because nobody my height ran the high hurdles, and I would need to invent an entirely new style.

"Why?" my father wanted to know. What drove me to do what other kids my age would have written off as an impractical pursuit?

"Because the coach said I can't do it. I'd like to show him that I can."

So began a few months of the self-discipline I carry to this day, in life, in founding a Silicon Valley microchip company without venture capital, in 37 years of business with only one unprofitable year.

My father and I built a pair of high hurdles. Every afternoon I was behind our house, practicing for hours. Dad would put a bottle cap on each hurdle, and my goal was to knock the cap off the bar without touching the homemade hurdle itself. That's quite a stunt since the bottle caps of that era measured perhaps a quarter of an inch thick. But mastering this taught me how to get the right lift in my jump without expending all my energy.

That last bit was important because my short-legged strides made running between hurdles impossible using the typical method. Hurdlers always launch with the same foot forward. They take three long strides between hurdles and then put the same foot up into the air each time. I had to take four shorter strides, forcing me to alternate my lead foot with each hurdle. Whereas everyone else running down the same 70 yards of track strengthened and stretched half of his body for peak performance, I had to double that effort. I also had to take advantage of my center of gravity and experience in sprinting to get ahead of the other runners at the start of the race. Sprinting, bilateral leaping, adding 25 percent more steps for the same distance—no wonder shorter fellows don't try this.

After months of drilling myself at home, I went to the track and told the coach I'd like to run the hurdles. It was time for the district finals, and tryouts were open to everybody. The coach—having seen me assault his hurdles before but not having seen my months of private preparation—flatly said no while making some excuse about interfering with the other runners, the ones he presumed had a chance to win without smashing his gear. I wasn't going to accept that answer because I knew I could do it. I bargained, suggesting that I run in the farthest lane. Separated from the other runners, if I flipped a hurdle, nobody would be harmed or even have his concentration thrown off. He relented, and I stepped into the blocks in the most remote lane, a fair distance from much taller boys with their long, reaching legs.

I beat every one of them.

This is the essence of the entrepreneurial spirit. If it looks like an impossible task—and running the high hurdles faster than the tall boys looked impossible—with determination, with practice you can do the impossible. You simply must find the discipline to do it.

When I founded Micrel—a Silicon Valley semiconductor devices company—in 1978, we did the supposedly impossible. Silicon Valley thrives on venture capital, yet we launched Micrel without any. Chip industry revenues and profits fluctuate wildly with technology adoption cycles, yet Micrel has been profitable from the very first year with only one exception: the year 2002, in the echo of the dot-com implosion. I never believed that we had to follow industry and Silicon Valley norms, many of which people said were essential. As with a shorter man running the high hurdles, nothing was impossible to me once I saw the objective, understood the barriers, and employed the discipline necessary to make it happen.

Discipline defines successful entrepreneurs. Their vision, their disbelief in failure, their love of doing things—even things they don't love—drives them to adopt discipline. Entrepreneurial discipline turns hurdles into exciting challenges, and no hurdle appears too high. Building a business comes with instilling the organization with the disciplines that are the foundation of corporate culture. Often an entrepreneur doesn't even understand that he is disciplined, and as a leader he transfers that discipline to everyone around him. Yet it is discipline that builds the business and fulfills the vision he has. In every entrepreneur, we see the following:

- **Focus:** Distractions are antithetic to entrepreneurs. They know in their hearts and minds what they want to create, and they find a way to create it. Stopping a focused entrepreneur is like trying to halt plate tectonics.
- **Short time frames:** Entrepreneurs are impatient by nature, but they also understand the value of timely innovation: what they fail to bring to market today will be brought to market by someone else tomorrow. Entrepreneurs move quickly to excite their customers while hamstringing their competitors.
- **Frugality:** Excesses of the dot-com era aside, great entrepreneurs build frugal organizations. Cash is king, and spending their own cash is less expensive than using investor money or bank loans. "Making do" is an entrepreneur's creed.
- **Being the best:** Second place is never where entrepreneurs envision themselves. For them, doing their personal best is a natural mode of operation, and they encourage everyone in the organization to live for the same standard of quality.

This last element may be the most important for entrepreneurs. Being the best at what one does—what makes an entrepreneur and her company different in the marketplace—becomes the source of corporate missions as well as operations. Someone in a commodity business may focus intently on cost minimization, and by being the best at cost controls she becomes the most profitable commodity vendor in that industry. Producing the most intuitive consumer electronics cemented Apple and Steven Jobs's fame. Being the best creates value, and businesspeople who are not willing to be their best never become true entrepreneurs.

Admiral Hyman Rickover knew this, and he stunned Jimmy Carter into believing it as well. Carter was an ensign at the U.S. Naval Academy at Annapolis. As graduation approached, he met with Rickover. Carter came into Rickover's office and, doing what any ensign would, stood while Rickover was focused on his work.

"Ensign Carter is reporting, sir," was how Carter's telling began. Rickover, sitting in his chair, left the young Carter standing. According to Carter, Rickover asked only one simple question: "Did you do your best?" Being a humble southern man, Carter demurred, saying, "No sir, I didn't always do my best."

Rickover spun around and said to Ensign Carter, "If not your best, why not?"

That story has stuck with me, and I have seen other entrepreneurs who act as if they had heard the story as well. Why not your best? Why not be *the* best? Why be satisfied with "I think I did okay" or "We're doing fine"? If not your best, why not?

Doing your best takes you outside the envelope called "average." It is what allowed Microsoft to take market from Ashton-Tate, Lotus 1-2-3, and WordPerfect. It wasn't necessarily that Microsoft was great but that those other companies were not the best. It wasn't that Ashton-Tate did not innovate with the dBase personal database product—once the best in the business—but that it did not strive to continue being the best. The same story can be told of thousands of Silicon Valley companies, once famous and now forgotten.

When stripped of overanalysis, discipline is simply overcoming the "natural man." Humans, like many other animals, are shaped by their environment, prone to limit risk and conserve energy. In nature this means looking for the low-hanging fruit and resting whenever possible. Humans advanced mainly because our brains evolved to the point where we could see beyond our villages and wonder what was over the horizon. We learned to suppress the urge to eat seeds because planting them produced greater abundance. Our intellect overcame the natural man, driving the start of civilization and planting the seeds of commerce.

Part of growing beyond the natural man involved doing things we didn't like to do. Napping away each afternoon sounds better than sweating in the fields while hoeing row after row and dropping tasty seeds into the dirt. But our ancestors did what they disliked to achieve their long-term vision of a full larder during long winters. This took our species one more step away from the natural man. We learned to love doing the things we did not love. We did the tough things first.

I kept this in mind when I went legally blind on the eve of Micrel's IPO.

We filed for an initial public offering (IPO) in October 1994, after 16 years of straight profitability and 4 recent years of steady high growth. The next month, while we were presenting to potential investors in London, my eyesight faded, making me legally blind. At first we hoped it was a transient condition, but it persisted. I traveled back to the United States, to the San Francisco Bay Area, and to the best specialists the University of California at San Francisco provided. The verdict was the same. My eyesight was failing, and it was not reversible.

Conventional wisdom—a by-product of consensus thinking by natural man—would have been to stall the IPO or for me to resign from my own company. Even if the IPO was allowed to proceed, many suggested I could not run Micrel afterward: the board of directors would insist on a fully sighted person commanding a newly public enterprise. Such in-the-box thinking is not a trait among entrepreneurs, certainly not with me. Yet I remained the CEO and chairman of the board 20 years later. To me the inconvenience of limited sight was the same as high hurdles: a challenge that could be overcome with the right discipline.

I thought about the daily activities of a CEO and recruited technology—as old as magnifying glasses and as modern as iPads—to facilitate work, interaction, communications, and leadership. Micrel did not slow or change course. Starting without venture capital, growing on our own cash flow, staying profitable every year but one, exceeding the quality that our engineer buyers demanded—they were all merely hurdles jumped by a company that knew it could do that by applying the necessary discipline.

An entrepreneur-led organization is like a gymnast, another pursuit of my youth. Gymnasts train every muscle of the body since they must compete in all events: steel rings, pommel horse, vaulting, parallel bars, horizontal (high) bars, and floor exercises. But without an alert mind and a healthy central nervous system, a physically trained body cannot walk—much less grab the rings, swinging toward the heavens and landing effortlessly. It could never dance across the mat, gyrate over a horse, or perform a Diamidov on the parallel bars. The body and mind of a gymnast or an enterprise must be trained, and it begins with the organization's mind . . . the entrepreneurial mind. Only then can the body be conditioned to perform at its best and perform consistently over time.

I still do handstands around the office, half blind and in my seventies. A disciplined body remembers how to do what it has been trained to do.

Doing the tough things first, knowing the challenges that are in the path of your mission, and tackling the large, complex, and boring ones first—having the discipline of taking care of your most significant roadblocks—is what separates those who achieve from those who do not. Nobody can be a successful entrepreneur without being willing and excited to find the biggest boulder and make it the first one you hammer into pebbles.

Your company is the body of your vision, and you, the entrepreneur, are the mind, eyes, and heart. In Part I of *Tough Things First*, you will learn about the mind, eyes, heart, and body of any company and how they are interrelated. In Part II, you will learn how applying organization discipline through culture, people processes, finances, and more trains a disciplined company body. If you have a vision for things that should be created and markets to conquer, your mind is ready to be disciplined for success. Once you own your vision and have the discipline to lead yourself, you will be ready to train the body: your organization.

TOUGH
THINGS
FIRST

BUSINESS AS A BODY: DISCIPLINING A BODY FROM HEAD TO FOOT

CHAPTER 1

The Brain

Standing naked in the bathroom of a cattle ranch office will make a person contemplate the value of self-discipline.

I was 19, and like many young men who had started college and seen a small part of the world, I thought I was smarter than most. Having grown up on a ranch in the beastly hot Imperial Valley and now a bored junior at Brigham Young University, I made the command decision to quit higher education. I had determination. I had talent. But I had little money and even less love for college and rigorous study. Taking time off to work and filling my pockets seemed like a great strategy.

After driving the 760 miles back home from Provo, I landed at our house in the town of El Centro, California. The ranch was farther down the road, but my mother—a schoolteacher who preferred the social amenities that even a small town provides—decided early in her marriage that the family would live not at the ranch but in the nearest burg of a suitable size.

"What are you doing home?" she asked, surprised to see me in the middle of a semester. After I told her about my decision to cancel my education, she asked, "Does your dad know that?"

Since I had gone directly to the house and Dad was working at the ranch, the answer was no.

"I think you should go tell him," she suggested in that tone mothers use when a suggestion is in fact a politely worded command.

I wasn't ready to do that, in no small part because I had traveled a fair distance solo. "Going to get some sleep right now," I informed my mother. "I've been driving all night." I then went to my room and flopped onto my bed. I started to drift toward sleep when my mother came to the door of my room to let me know that my father was on the telephone. "How's that?" I asked, foggy-headed and confused.

"I called him," my mother replied. "And I told him about your decision to quit college."

I asked why reporting my personal life decision was so urgent.

"Because he's my husband and he's your dad."

I struggled out of bed and back into my travel-scented clothes, stumbling down to the telephone. My father, a man of succinct dialogue, said only four words: "Get out here now." Then he hung up.

After driving to the ranch, I met my father in the operations office. Instead of the usual "Hello," "How are you?" or "Are you hungry?" he simply asked me for the keys to my car. This didn't make any sense to me at all, as it was unrelated to college, work, or anything else in my newly forged life plan. "Because it's my car," he said when I asked him why he needed the keys.

"What do you mean it's your car? I bought it."

"No, it isn't *yours,*" he said, punctuating his reply. "You haven't paid me for it. You may be making payments to me, but you haven't paid for it. It is still mine, and I want the keys."

I tossed the keys to "my" car on his desk, suspecting this was not the end of our discussion.

"Now I want your shoes."

I started to object until he said, "Because they're my shoes."

"What do you mean, 'your shoes'? I paid for them."

"Yes, but you still owe me for them. Because you live at the house, and even though you may have bought them with your money, they're still my shoes."

I gave him the footgear. He then demanded—one at a time— my socks, my pants, and my shirt. It was getting embarrassing. A working ranch employs many people, quite a few of them women, who tended to circulate through the office in which I was now nearly nude. A ranch's office is much like a kitchen in a large family: it is the hub of all activity. When he demanded that I hand over my underwear, I strenuously objected.

"Go into the bathroom and then hand your underpants out to me."

I did as I was told. I handed my wadded-up BVDs through the barely cracked bathroom door and was now standing stark naked in the public restroom of the ranch. Hardened cowboys came and went, openly amused to find the owner's son standing bare-skinned in such a place. I grabbed a fistful of paper towels from over the sink and tried with limited success to wrap them around my most personal anatomical regions.

That was nine-thirty in the morning. I languished there well past lunchtime. The hired hands and even some visitors came and went. Several laughed at the sight of a young man adorned with wadded paper pacing a public bathroom. I would nod, trying to be as nonchalant as the circumstances allowed, but that only caused them to snicker or laugh aloud before leaving. I'm sure I was the talk of the entire ranch, if not the county, by five o'clock that afternoon when my dad knocked on the bathroom door.

"I'm ready to lock the office up. You're going to have to find some other place to stay."

"What do you mean?" I was terrified. This odd punishment was suddenly getting serious.

"I can't let you stay here because I'm going to lock up. You may want to call one of your friends or somebody to come get you."

I was less worried about transportation than I was about being transported au naturel.

Dad was blunt: "You're going to go out in the world like you came into it. You entered this family with nothing, you go out with nothing. You want to be on your own, you're on your own . . . but you're going to start with nothing just like you did when you arrived."

"That's not fair," I retorted.

"You have a choice. You either go back to school or leave."

"That's not much of a choice."

"I'm not trying to give you one."

Faced with a stark set of limited options, I agreed to resume my education. My clothing and car keys were tossed into the men's room.

"I'm going to go home," I said, trying to exert some remnant of independence, "and get some rest before I go back. I haven't slept for almost twenty-four hours . . . and not only that, but I have to pack myself a lunch for when I leave tomorrow."

"Your lunch is already in your car," Dad said while I was still pulling on my pants. "Your mom packed it for you already. You're going to leave *now*. When you get too tired to drive, pull off and get some sleep."

I drove for five hours, pulled off the road, slept in the car, and then gunned it the rest of the way to Provo. Less than 48 hours after making the decision to quit school, I was back in class.

I didn't love school. It was tough. Yet getting a college education was the direction my father insisted I take, at least while he was financing any part of my existence. The benefits of a college education were obvious, but I lacked the self-discipline to see it through, and Dad wisely provided very clear incentives to gain that discipline.

That is the essence of discipline: doing the tough things first. When I wanted to run the high hurdles, I did the hard and unpleasant work of physically training my body to succeed at the sport. To get a college degree, I did the hard and occasionally unpleasant work of studying, researching, and taking tests.

Actually, it is a bit more involved. Any underachiever can blunder through a task with lackluster results. I define discipline as doing what you don't like doing *and doing it well*—having the determination, no matter how difficult a task is, to do it correctly. To do everything superbly is the end result of discipline on a personal level or for an enterprise. The task could be as complex as designing a critical microchip component for a manned spacecraft or as simple as cutting the grass.

With respect to the grass, my younger brother and I were charged with mowing the yard. Yard work isn't entertaining, and in those quainter times we had only a push lawn mower, gas-powered mowers not being commonplace or affordable for a frugal ranching family in the California desert. To mow the yard well, I decided to make my brother cut the grass in one direction and again at a perpendicular angle. He'd mow it one way and then had to cut the grass once more at 90 degrees. This assured that the lawn was neatly manicured. More work—especially on those blistering hot Imperial Valley days—but perfect, uniform results.

Did he hate doing double duty? Yes, he did, and says so to this day. I hated going back to school. But discipline requires doing what you don't like to achieve the things you want. The reason most would-be entrepreneurs with great ideas and plenty of fire in the belly fail is that they never really start. On the list of steps to achieving one's goal, there are one or more really tough things that must be done. People often skip projects not because most of the steps are hard—most are easy. They forsake the opportunity because one really difficult or unpleasant task looms before them. It is the mountain they don't want to climb.

But if Moses had not scaled Mount Nebo, he never would have seen the Promised Land.

Very few people enjoy lifting heavy objects, yet early each morning every 24 Hour Fitness Center is clogged with people hoisting hunks of pig iron and trying to lift more than they did before. They do this day after day, week after week, year after year. They endure the temporary discomfort of weight lifting to satisfy their desire for athletic ability, physical beauty, or health. They have discipline. Concert pianists practice their scales every day before rehearsing or composing and have done so every day of every decade since their first piano lesson as a child. They have discipline. CEOs review monthly inventory and sales reports despite having hired people more than capable of understanding the metrics because they want to feel the pulse of the company and be aware of warning signs. They have discipline.

For true entrepreneurs—people who have a vision and drive themselves and their organizations relentlessly toward that vision— a peculiar thing occurs. They begin to love doing what they don't love. They develop the desire to do even the mundane well, because the joy is in the execution that leads to their vision. An entrepreneur explores the scope of bookkeeping just as weight lifters develop an endorphin rush when they lift. The entrepreneur masters public speaking despite originally being a shy technologist, and the pianist finds ways of putting his signature trills on even the simple pentatonic scale. The entrepreneur walks the factory floor, eyeing everything and talking to everyone. A short-in-stature hurdle runner grins with every barrier she leaves untouched.

A quirk shared by entrepreneurs is the satisfaction of doing well what they don't like doing at all. They love unlovable tasks because of their desire to achieve and learn. They look back on the tough things they did the way a rancher looks back on a mile of newly strung barbed wire and thinks, "Yeah. I did that. I didn't want to do it, but I did it." Challenge and achievement become their own reward. More important, though, entrepreneurs constantly learn and gain satisfaction from everything they do. Doing all the tough tasks—whether the intricate discovery of new means for etching silicon wafers or mastering the interaction between inventory and holding cost—fulfills the common and fundamental personality trait of entrepreneurs.

In the process, they learn to love what they don't love.

The entrepreneur—innately desirous of understanding—is the brain in the corporate body. The brain is a complex machine, the original supercomputer, unmatched by technology. It receives millions of bits of discrete data every second, makes thousands of decisions in the same amount of time, and sends instructions to every corner of the body. If the brain were not involved, the body would fail. Arms and legs would flap uncontrollably. The skeleton would stumble and fall. The entire organism would die. Within the corporate body there must be an entrepreneurial brain that orchestrates the flow of blood, nutrition, electrical impulses, muscle contractions, and breathing. It may be a founder in a two-person start-up or the CEO of a multinational conglomerate. The brain must exist and be disciplined for the body to survive, much less thrive.

The corporate mind and the mind of the entrepreneur are no different from the muscles in the human body. They have to be trained in a certain way. If you need strong back muscles, you have to train your back muscles. If you need strong biceps, you train those biceps. Each, however, needs to be trained in a certain way to perform a certain function.

In disciplining the mind, training requires organizing memory and thinking like a filing cabinet. You know where the information you are storing resides, and you can pull it at will. The ability to think and retrieve information comes from repetition, just as huge biceps come from doing many preacher curls. You can't do one rep and expect to grow big biceps, and you can't organize corporate thinking by talking about it once at a staff meeting. The more reps you do, the more responsive your muscle or memory becomes.

This is where entrepreneurial leadership and corporate culture become the fundamental wiring of the corporate brain. The more you review in your mind a particular principle and the more frequently you act in accordance with that principle, the more mental muscle memory you build. As an entrepreneur exercises his mind to accomplish tasks at will, he also communicates to his organization the discipline of similar mental exercise. Whether it is a policy, procedure, guiding principle, or corporate motto, the more it is repeated, the more the corporate body responds effortlessly.

Where some entrepreneurs go astray is in forcing their infant company bodies to run marathons. Nothing is born fully formed. Humans cannot fend for themselves until they are teenagers. A novice pianist cannot play both the left and the right hand at the first lesson. As the human mind, through repetition, develops one's ability, that ability assumes nearly autonomic activity, freeing the mind to learn the next, collaborative action. Many new musicians tell me they cannot sing and play guitar simultaneously because the mind is focused on the new activity of forming chords and strumming in time. Yet every rock star, blues singer, and songwriter who accompanies herself was in that same limited state when she started. At some point in time, they mastered playing simple chords without looking at the left hand or thinking about how to form each chord. After a while, hammers and pulls are incorporated and also become automatic. A new gymnast is not coordinated until his mind studies and memorizes each action in a routine and then through repetition commands each muscle to execute that routine.

Companies are like gymnasts. When they are gangly in their younger years, each action is an attempt to master a move, whether it is their marketing messages, their research and development activities, or their technical support services. Over time, as the entrepreneur in charge receives corporate neurological feedback and the results of each action are studied and refined, the company changes from flailing student to graceful master of itself.

It is the paced training of the entrepreneurial mind and then the corporate mind that smooths the transition from an awkward start-up to a robust business. Don't try to take on too much at once. Don't try to play both the right hand and the left hand parts of a concerto during your first recital, and don't try to sell to the world during a beta test. All you're going to achieve is frustration. Think instead of learning line upon line, precept upon precept, and storing knowledge in the corporate muscle memory by repetition. The more organized your mind is and the more organized a corporate mind is, the more responsive to changing markets and economies each becomes.

If this sounds monotonous, you may not be ready for entrepreneurial pursuits or for leading an organization. Any group of people working toward a common goal requires the discipline of focusing on a goal, repeating policy, and adjusting as it learns. This requires a fair bit of repetition at all levels and a great deal of repetition at the top. If you can't stand doing that, you will never become great. That repetitive effort takes discipline simply to stick to a principle, and when all is said and done, corporate culture, policy, procedures, and the like, are all sets of principles that need to be practiced the way a gymnast practices each move in a routine. Once you achieve that mental discipline, you earn the muscle memory that allows you or your company to execute that principle at will and then move on to mastering the next pillar. It all begins with the mind, the entrepreneur's mind in particular.

Goals help make principles meaningful to everyone in the organization, and this is part of the process of instilling discipline in the corporate mind. I learned this because of California's byzantine system for allocating water. California has farmers and ranchers in the former deserts of the Imperial Valley, and cattle there drink from water sources allocated by the government. I got a driver's license when I was 13 because I had to drive to the ranch at night and get our water, which served a very real goal.

The ditch master gave us our allocation, but because water flows only so fast down the canals, not everyone can draw his or her water from nine to five. We rotated, and ditch masters came to your water gate at specified times of the day and night. If you were not there to meet the ditch master, you did not get your water. Crops died, animals could not be fed, farms and ranches went bankrupt. Pulling water was a crucial duty.

So at age 13, certified with a California driver's license, I would cruise out to meet the ditch master at eleven o'clock in the evening. For two to three hours, I would stay with the ditch master, making sure we got every drop allotted to us, finally getting home at two o'clock in the morning before rising again at five to get to school on time.

The goal was survival. No water, no crops, no livestock, no money, no ranch. It was a very simple mission that everyone in the family understood. If I didn't pull our water, my family would suffer. We all saw the goal of a thriving family ranch, knew our roles, and did our jobs as diligently as I pulled water. Corporations are no different. The company, or at least the entrepreneur, has a goal or a vision. When entrepreneurs make that vision plain to everyone they hire, everyone works in a fashion that drives toward that goal. By codifying principles that guide action—the way an old patriarch's principles lead a family ranch operation—the entrepreneur guides the actions of all the employees without the burden of directly micromanaging them.

Foremost, though, it requires the discipline of doing tough things first, or as Stephen Covey describes it, getting the big rocks out of the way early. In my ranching youth, I could not have said, "I'll go pull water after breakfast." The mechanics of desert ranching in southernmost California did not offer that luxury. I had to develop the discipline to stay up late, drive into the hinterlands where the head gates lay, understand water allocation and measurement, and keep myself on site until our water was secured.

We all have seen the outcome of an undisciplined mind, whether it is the lackluster employee, the ne'er-do-well cousin, or the easily tempted alcoholic. An undisciplined mind leads to idleness at best and decay at worst. This applies to organizations as well. If the entrepreneur fails to inculcate his teams with the mental discipline to do well and to think creatively, the organization as a whole will stumble through its existence and probably die young.

Traditional Silicon Valley thinking says that an entrepreneur is a "big picture guy" who should not "get lost" in the details but instead delegate details to specialists. The correct thinking is quite different: true entrepreneurs dive into the details of every aspect of their businesses. They ask questions until they understand everything: product, finances, operations, marketing, and sales. An intense desire to know all the factors involved in the success of the enterprise is the true entrepreneurs' creed.

Creating and maintaining organizational discipline requires the CEO to involve herself in the details of every function of the business. Leaving the details to specialized and more qualified people is akin to disconnecting the brain from the body—pulling out the central nervous system. Without the input a brain receives from every point in the body, warning signs of distress, illness, or injury would be ignored and the body would suffer accordingly. The CEO is the brain in the body of the organization and must receive sufficient and unfiltered signals from every appendage and every vital organ.

An entrepreneur needs information about whether her business is running properly. She does not need to know if every *i* was dotted on every proposal, nor does she need to understand why the last batch of silicon wafers had a marginally higher defect rate. But she does need to create and constantly monitor key indicators of the state of the corporate body to detect when its health might become jeopardized. She needs to see not only financial numbers in a spreadsheet but also whether the R&D department is struggling, whether tech support is overloaded, and when customer satisfaction trends negatively. Seeing such things personally is as vital as a human brain receiving pain signals from the site of a newly formed tumor.

One example of needing direct input is in technical support, a standard function in Silicon Valley. One poor measure some companies use to monitor the "effectiveness" of a tech support organization is how quickly cases are closed. In theory, case resolution is a sign of a tech support team resolving customer problems rapidly, which satisfies customers. But it also provides incentive to a tech support team manager—whose bonus check and future employment may hinge on this metric—to artificially close cases, leaving customer needs unfulfilled. If an entrepreneurial CEO simply relied on statistical analysis of case closing time frames, he might miss the fact that unhappy customers, abandoned by the CEO's tech support organization, are creating a poor brand image in the market. Silicon Valley learned this the hard way in the early part of this century when it outsourced support services overseas without properly managing the process.

The walking-around principle—a management invention credited to Hewlett-Packard's founders—is one tool CEOs have for getting necessary bodily feedback to detect organizational health problems or confirm good corporate fitness. Every CEO should routinely get out of his office and visit each department and working group so that he understands the problems that they face. He should meet with them as groups, engage employees one on one, and drop in on birthday celebrations. The details lie outside the CEO's office, and the Devil sleeps in the details. The CEO must keep the Devil awake and moving along.

One problem the entrepreneur faces is understanding the difference between transient symptoms and authentic diseases within the body of the organization. If she pays attention to every signal from every part of the organization and treats them all as equally important, each bad signal looks like an emergency room–worthy illness. Worried about the success of her company, an entrepreneur can become a hypochondriac, treating every production exception and financial shift as a sign of death. This is where management by walking around helps the CEO. Understanding how things work helps her correctly judge the importance and severity of the information she receives and thus make the right decision about what to do. If a CEO relied only on filtered input, he might slough off bad information just as an obese person might ignore that first tightness in the chest. A CEO who walks about might recognize instead the first sign of a heart attack. But the inverse applies: being exposed to the subtle shifts and day-to-day vagaries of each business component allows a CEO to understand that the chest tightness might simply be corporate indigestion and should be waited out until the next monthly financial reports.

Some entrepreneurs believe that the right way to manage an organization is to surround themselves with bright people and let them handle the details. This is like a person with five brains. He may have a healthy and vigorous body, but either the five brains try forcing the body to run in many different directions at once or he argues with himself and runs nowhere. The latter condition is far too common and is completely antithetical to entrepreneurial endeavors.

Surrounding yourself with bright people is wise but can lead to analysis paralysis or, worse yet, conventional thinking.

If an entrepreneur surrounds himself with smart people but fails to create a culture of free thinking, he will only receive the collective thinking of his inner circle. By definition, collective thinking is in-the-box thinking. Two heads may be better than one, but groups also discuss, debate, and jell around consensus—the average of all their thinking—seeking the norm or the middle.

Alternatively, they may sink into overanalysis as they second-guess one another and themselves. Decision-making processes become slower because each group seeks either to prove it is right or to minimize its personal risk in being wrong. The group tries to discourage outlier team members, the people still thinking outside of any box. Once this group of otherwise bright people has succeeded in finding the middle, the average, the predictable, everybody hunkers down and quits taking risks. It is safer to stay inside the box. A strong entrepreneurial leader must lead in these situations. It is better to take the reins in hand and pick a direction than to slump into corporate inaction.

When an entrepreneur receives too much filtered information, the head of the organizational body can get overwhelmed. When top management becomes paralyzed by constant circular analysis, the body goes into shock because it fails to receive instructions from the brain. A brain-dead body lasts for a short time on autonomic impulses, but soon enough the vital organs fail and the body dies. So too with organizations in which the CEO's cadre prevents action. The CEO needs the help of her top management team and board of directors, but she cannot rely solely on their input. She must receive additional input directly from every corner of the company and in sufficient detail to make informed decisions.

Heart attacks, angina, and strokes share some symptoms. If a patient knew only the symptoms of a heart attack, he might misdiagnose a stroke he was having. Such a misdiagnosis might lead to the wrong first-aid treatment or, worse, incorrect long-term treatments and medications. Similarly, top advisors to an entrepreneur might provide a diagnosis that is based on their understanding of the symptoms, and a CEO who is not actively in touch with his entire organization might allow those advisors to argue endlessly about the symptoms and what actions to take. Fully involved CEOs quickly understand where symptoms emanate from, when multiple warning signs from different parts of the corporate body are related, and whether the accumulated set of symptoms requires tweaking the corporate culture or pivoting within the market.

The entrepreneurial brain is no less complex than a real human brain and must be trained to deal with stimulus and signals coming from the corporate body. There are eight principles of a disciplined entrepreneurial mind. If you are launching a company, if you have a vision and passion, these are the areas where you need to train your mind and then reflect that training throughout your organization.

AN ENTREPRENEUR HAS SOME VISION FOR HIS OR HER LIFE AND BUSINESS THAT IS NOT FOCUSED ON FINANCIAL GAIN.

If you have a vision of what your company will do and know that there is limited time to accomplish the core mission, you are not shaken by small fluctuations in the business or the market. When you have your eyes firmly on where you want to take the company, the mechanisms reveal themselves. However, if you're focused only on money, as too many Silicon Valley entrepreneurs appear to be, your vision is impaired—you quit focusing on your mission and focus only on cash. You lose sight of what you originally wanted, which was a long-term pursuit, and instead erratically chase short-term monetary problems.

At Micrel, I never really worried about how much money I would make, though I engineered my fortune to rely on Micrel's success, and that kept me fully engaged over the decades. I knew that all my efforts ultimately would accomplish what we wanted: the original Micrel vision. By not worrying if I would become a millionaire, I kept my attention riveted on where Micrel would fit into the microchip market, how my employees would prosper, and what legacy I could leave for others.

This is important on a spiritual level as well. CEOs who fixate on money tend to lose sight of the real purpose of life: their mission, the thrill of accomplishment, the joy of building a company that employs many people. Their money obsession can also lead to personal problems ranging from alcoholism to divorce, because the focus on money detracts from the focus on people and life.

It is the same way with gymnastics. There's really no money in the sport aside from becoming an Olympic athlete and earning a few temporary product endorsement deals. The entire point of being a gymnast is the desire to fearlessly perform astounding physical feats gracefully and demonstrate just how skilled you are in that particular discipline. The same thing applies to being a singer, for the odds of ever making good money in the music business are low enough to churn out an endless supply of cocktail lounge song stylists. But if a gymnast or singer focused primarily on money, she would be constantly distracted to the point of never training completely or might become unfocused in the middle of the performance. At the end of their careers, these people might have a few dollars in their pockets but would have missed the joy of the journey. They would have robbed themselves of their own humanity by choosing the wrong priority.

Silicon Valley venture capitalists don't help entrepreneurs in this regard, because their focus is always on money.

Thankfully, for true entrepreneurs, money is rarely the issue. Entrepreneurs are calculated risk takers. Not having money is a risk they understand but one that does not trouble them to the point of distraction. To entrepreneurs, accomplishment—the art of doing— is the driving motivation. To them it is like breathing or eating food. It is a need as opposed to a desire. It has been said that writers do not write because they want to—they do so because they have to, to sate their addiction. Entrepreneurs don't invent products or organize, manage, and grow businesses because they want to; they do it because those are steps on the path to accomplishment.

There is a classic story concerning Socrates. One of his students kept bugging him about how to obtain knowledge. Socrates told the student to meet him on the shoreline at six o'clock the next morning, promising to show him how to learn.

The eager student was there at five-thirty. When Socrates arrived, he took the student out into the ocean until the water was chest-high on both of them. Socrates then shoved the student's head underwater, keeping it submerged until the student was flailing his arms, fighting his instructor, and finally breaking free to gasp a lungful of air.

Socrates asked the student, "What did you want more than anything else while your head was underwater?"

The wild-eyed and panting student replied, "I wanted air!"

Socrates said, "When you want knowledge as much as you want air, you'll find a way to get it."

That insatiable desire is what defines entrepreneurs. To them, accomplishing is the end, and they are driven to find ways to achieve their goals. Need drives them into a realm beyond mere desire.

Desire can be purely material and temporal. You can want love but live without it. Yet you *need* air and cannot long survive in its absence. When you need accomplishment, you tend to have a driven approach to solving a problem. Desire to achieve is fundamental to being an entrepreneur.

AN ENTREPRENEUR ALWAYS THINKS OUTSIDE THE BOX.

Ponder the in- and out-of-the-box metaphor. A box is a cell where a person is surrounded on all six sides. Everyone inside of the box sees exactly the same thing all the time. They are prisoners in a cell of aggregate group observation and thus average group thinking.

Entrepreneurs perpetually explore the outside of the box. Some entrepreneurs are driven by curiosity, and curiosity has always been the force behind pioneers and explorers. Some entrepreneurs have been nearly psychic in their intuitive grasp of the possible, but most are merely pathfinders, examining what is and what might be and finding the path from one to the other. By peeking out of the box, around a corner, over the lid, they see the bits and pieces of the possible. Once their vision is firmly set on what is possible, they drive relentlessly toward it. John Kennedy saw that it was possible to put men on the moon and then instilled an entire nation with the desire to accomplish that mission.

I have been awarded multiple patents, and I conceptualized and sold the first wafer steppers, a staple machine in the semiconductor industry. At Micrel alone, I have landed over 11 patents, and the Micrel headquarters lobby is walled with all the patents the company has earned. You are given a patent when you conceive of something so unique that the government is willing to give you a temporary monopoly on the invention in exchange for your sharing your genius with the world. At least for engineering and scientific pursuits, a patent confirms that you saw something other people could not see. Whether it is divine inspiration or merely peeking around enough corners on the outside of the box to understand what is possible, it is unconventional thinking that showcases the entrepreneurial mind.

Entrepreneurial vision is essential when the idea an entrepreneur has is ahead of the market it serves. Many more challenges are added to the list when an idea does not yet have all the necessary support: no supply chain, no market demand. Entrepreneurs see the goal and how a product or service fulfills that goal and then drive the product, suppliers, and customers toward adoption. When I conceived of the wafer stepper, the industry was not ready for it. The wafer stepper created microchips of a smaller size and with greater tolerance than was needed at that time. But I also foresaw that in my lifetime technology would pack millions of transistors into the same physical space that single transistors once occupied. The market as a whole was not ready for my invention, but it would be; the trends were already in place, and competitive pressures would drive semiconductor manufacturing to the point where wafer steppers were essential.

AN ENTREPRENEUR IS HIGHLY CREATIVE.

It isn't enough to be outside the box in which everyone else lives. You can be an outside-the-box thinker yet never see how to connect the disparate concepts and technologies you encounter. Steven Jobs saw that once you defaulted everything, including text, to be a graphical element, everything could be elegantly simplified—and nothing defines Apple more than elegant simplicity.

An entrepreneur's mind is such that he sees what can be connected but also sees the value in the connections. That is an intrinsically creative process. It is also creative to deny the deniers—the people who hear your idea and say, "So what? Nobody will want that." The creation of value involves being outside the box enough to see the possible, understand why it is valuable, and then communicate that value to investors, employees, and buyers.

Being an entrepreneur also requires the wisdom to know what isn't worth pursuing. Scan the U.S. patent database and you will find many curious things with absolutely no value. The inventions were creative, but they devised technologies nobody wanted . . . *ever*. There is a distinction between being creative, which does not require one to be an entrepreneur, and being an entrepreneur, which requires being creative.

Part of entrepreneurial creativity involves creating the boring bits—doing the tough stuff first. In the heyday of the dot-com explosion, Webvan came to life and acquired over a billion dollars in capital. It crashed while others have run with its basic idea. Webvan decided to explode onto the market and spend its money in an attempt to instantly be a fully formed nationwide entity. It lacked the creativity and discipline to frugally build the end-to-end infrastructure required to fulfill its vision.

AN ENTREPRENEUR ALWAYS BELIEVES HE OR SHE WILL SUCCEED.

Franklin Roosevelt famously said, "We have nothing to fear but fear itself." Entrepreneurs only fear doubt, and true entrepreneurs are good at reducing it. By lessening doubt, they become fearless and never disbelieve their chance of success.

A young acquaintance of mine called one day. A few years after starting his business, he received a letter from a lawyer unjustly threatening a lawsuit that would require him to exit a segment of his targeted market. He had become consumed by this issue: how unjust it was and what the ramifications could be. "I love suing guys like you," I said. "Why don't you just get out of the business?" This was not a sincere suggestion but a way of illustrating that his fear was interfering with his vision and his mission. It was keeping him from succeeding. "Whoever these lawyers are, they have no idea of the kind of pit bull they have to deal with if they go after you. Nothing will happen to you. Now go and run your business." He did, and he prevailed.

Reducing doubt is a mental discipline like any other. If you enter a room that is pitch black, what do you do? You stop because you have doubts about where you are and whether you are about to smash your shin into the coffee table. You don't charge into the room because you doubt your knowledge concerning what and where the obstacles are. Your doubt causes you to freeze, and this is what keeps most people from achieving what they desire. Doubt restricts your ability to move. The more doubtful you are, the more slowly you move and the less convinced you are about where you're going.

If you have a conviction or insight into how to understand and work around obstacles, you can transverse the dark room or a new market with ease. The entrepreneur removes doubt by exploring. She turns each obstacle into a challenge and studies it with the same passion with which she holds her vision. Entrepreneurs are born not with reckless abandon but with the drive to turn the unknown into the known and by doing so to reduce or eliminate doubt.

In this absence of doubt, entrepreneurs take away the worry that they might fail. Success is the absence of failure, and through the absence of a sense of failure, they believe they're going to succeed.

Entrepreneurs never give up.

Since entrepreneurs disbelieve in their likelihood of failure, they remain focused on how to succeed. They know where they are headed, know they can navigate the dark rooms of markets, vendors, supply chains, regulations, and more. They never get in the mindset of stopping. In the absence of doubt and distraction, they become relentless in the pursuit of their vision (sadly, for some, to the exclusion of family, friends, and country).

Entrepreneurs never say, "It's too dark; I don't know where I am." They think instead that the door they want to walk through is somewhere, and so they need to find a flashlight, build a fire, crawl carefully until they find a wall . . . anything that gets them to the door and to their goal. They proceed with conviction because they understand why they are moving forward and know that they have the ability to figure out a means for getting there. They advance more expeditiously than people who have doubt, who thus give up before they even begin.

There's an old saying that goes, "Begin; the rest is easy." An entrepreneur begins precisely because he believes the rest of it is easy or at least doable. Writers may complain that getting started is difficult—that staring at a blank page is intimidating—but once they get the first sentence written, the rest flows naturally. The biggest problem would-be entrepreneurs have is getting started, and it all comes from doubt.

Entrepreneurs attract success.

Entrepreneurs *are* successful, because to an entrepreneur success is merely overcoming failure. Even Edison, one of the great inventive entrepreneurs in history, said, "I have [never] failed. I've just found 10,000 ways that won't work."

Success is not like a lottery or a spinning roulette wheel. That is luck. Success is overcoming failure: identifying obstacles, finding ways around them, and *pushing forward*. Left to their natural state, things fail. A fruit rots if you let it sit on a shelf, but we long ago discovered that you can blanch and freeze that piece of fruit and enjoy it later. We overcame an inherent limitation of nature.

One by-product of the entrepreneur's predisposition to success is that he attracts success. John Madden once said that winning is a great deodorant—if you are successful, if you win, other people will come to also be successful regardless of other factors. An entrepreneur can face a lot of problems, but as long as he is winning, people ignore those difficulties. Because entrepreneurs are in the mode of winning, people will tolerate any problems they face and help them overcome those problems. When they believe a leader or a company will fail, they tend to give up. Success breeds success, whereas failure breeds failure.

ENTREPRENEURS HAVE A LASER FOCUS.

A laser is a beam of light with one frequency. If you could hear a laser beam, it would sound like a single key pressed on a music synthesizer, not the whole band playing along. Lasers also have a light spectrum associated with them that allows the beam to travel great distances. Lasers have a higher intensity at their destination point, whereas noncoherent light spreads out over distance. The more light spreads out, the more scattered it gets and the shorter becomes the distance at which it will illuminate anything. Laser beams remain intact all the way to the point of impact.

Focused impact over time and distance embodies entrepreneurial laserlike quality. It illuminates whatever goal you want to accomplish over a longer period. It's not short. The field of view is not scattered. Entrepreneurs see their goals and, like a laser, reach them without fading, without scattering, without interference from other light sources. Anyone distracted by peripheral stuff is not an entrepreneur. The ability to focus all of one's energy on that one spot—that vision one has—requires laserlike properties.

An entrepreneur must maintain control of the business.

Traditional Silicon Valley thinking says that an entrepreneur gets the "smart" people together, gets venture capital (VC) funding, and orchestrates team functions. The correct thinking is that an entrepreneur drives his own agenda. He wins others over to his way of thinking. He seeks no VC funding so that he can retain control of his vision. It is not about money.

One of the saddest aspects of Silicon Valley culture is the rush to riches. There is nothing wrong with being rich, but trading control of the business—the machine for obtaining one's vision—for money goes against the entrepreneurial mindset. Yes, there are serial entrepreneurs who know in advance that they will exit sooner rather than later to pursue other ideas and thus are willing to relinquish control of the business to investors. But in doing so, they relinquish control of their vision and may not be properly called entrepreneurs.

Assume you are barreling down a crowded freeway at rush hour and the person who owns the car you are driving is in the passenger seat. She says, "I own this car, and I'm going to drive now," before grabbing the wheel and sticking her legs between yours and onto the gas pedal. If you were heading to your parents' house, she may want to go to the bar instead. You might believe slowing down a bit is wise given changing traffic patterns, but she could floor it and shift into high gear. You might see the freight train at the rapidly approaching railroad crossing while she is fiddling with the radio dial.

Regardless of the specific outcome, you are not going to reach the destination you chose when you turned the ignition key.

A car and a business should have only one driver to avoid crashing and burning. In an airplane, the pilot has access to everything: the ailerons, the rudder, the elevator, the flaps, the landing gear. If he does not have access to everything, he is not in control of the aircraft and everyone aboard will probably perish. Could you land an airplane without being in control of the rudder, flaps, and engine? Could you navigate the car home if someone else had the wheel, a third person had the brakes, and another person had siphoned the gas?

If you cannot maintain control of your company, you cannot succeed in reaching the goal, the vision you have in mind. With early equity investors you may think you have control when in fact you really don't. If a venture capitalist can tell you how to run your business, you no longer own the steering wheel and probably will never reach the goals you had. If they have enough influence, if they own enough of your start-up, they not only can tell you how to run your company, they can dismiss you from it.

And they will, eventually.

LESSONS

- Learn to love what you don't love doing or it will never get done.
- There is no discipline unless there is self-discipline.
- Do everything well; doing less than your best is close to not doing it at all.
- True entrepreneurs love doing the tough and mundane things because it completes their vision.

- If the corporate mind—the entrepreneur—is weak, the corporate body will stumble.
- Entrepreneurs train the corporate body and never ask it to do more than it is ready for.
- Repetition—policies, procedures, principles—is the foundation of training the corporate body.
- Details intrigue and excite entrepreneurs; they love to know how the entire company works.
- Management by walking around prevents every problem from looking like a crisis.
- Surrounding yourself with bright people does not eliminate the need for details.
- By nature, entrepreneurs think outside the box and cause others to do so.
- Entrepreneurs always believe they will succeed, and that is the primary force behind their success.
- Entrepreneurs have a laserlike focus.
- Venture capital can be the antithesis of entrepreneurialism and success.

CHAPTER 2

The Eyes

Among all bodily senses, eyesight is the most essential. I lost mine shortly before Micrel issued its initial public offering.

I was in London on a leg of our IPO road show, in which Micrel senior management was engaging investors in the last months before we went public. We were in a restaurant when it started. The menu appeared to have little pieces missing, though everything around it looked right. At first I thought the menu had a printing error. I asked the guy seated next to me how his menu looked, and he said it was fine, and so I took his menu, and it looked just as poorly printed as mine.

I muddled through ordering dinner and wrote off the experience as a transient affair. But the next morning when I faced the mirror to shave, my eyesight was foggy. As with the disjointed menu, what was in the center of my field of view was haywire, though the periphery was still working well enough. At first I wiped the mirror off, thinking that something was wrong with the glass; perhaps an antifog coating had not been evenly applied. When wiping away nonexistent steam didn't work, I had my first indication that my eyes were the problem.

It was retinal vein occlusion, and this was not my first encounter with it. This "stroke in the eye" destroys tissues—in this case the light-sensing tissues of the retina—by robbing them of blood supply, and it had taken away a good deal of my left eye's vision in 1968. Perhaps it was the limited scientific knowledge of that era, but doctors told me that it was highly unlikely that I would experience retinal vein occlusion in my right eye, much less a quarter of a century later. Even with my left eye hampered, I drove, piloted airplanes, and created and grew Micrel to become an IPO-worthy enterprise. My right eye compensated, testing at 20/15 until it too had the eyeball's equivalent of a hemorrhagic stroke.

I stubbornly assumed that this was a transient condition until it wasn't. I needed to know what was happening because it had an immediate impact on Micrel, our IPO, and thus our employees. I called home to find the right specialists, then flew back, still making business stops in Minneapolis and Denver. All the while my eyesight got worse and worse. By the time I arrived home in Silicon Valley, my eyesight had deteriorated to about 20/100, and it dropped to 20/400 within another week.

Time being a patient physician, my eyesight has returned to 20/150. I ride to work with other people, have given up flying, and have employed technology to compensate for the significant loss of the most important bodily sense.

But none of this slowed down the Micrel IPO.

Impaired eyesight does not impair entrepreneurial vision. The entrepreneur cannot see everything all at once but develops the discipline to see what needs to be seen in a context that keeps the brain fully informed at all times. This requires acquiring the discipline to focus intently, filter the unnecessary, and maintain the correct perspective.

Focus

When Bill Gates and Warren Buffett agree on something, it is probably important.

In her book *The Snowball*, Alice Schroeder reported that both Gates and Buffett considered focus the single most important factor behind their success. Ignore great timing, good luck, and general business savvy. Focus made two of America's best-known billionaires. The same thing applies to all successful entrepreneurs: a nearly obsessive focus on their vision and their companies.

Focus is the most important yet the trickiest element in entrepreneurial eyesight. Focus has both long- and short-term properties as well as the seemingly impossible ability to keep a big-picture perspective while being intimate with the details of a company. Acquiring and keeping focus is essential to entrepreneurs, and I daresay that nobody becomes a true entrepreneur without it. Nobody builds an enterprise from scratch without the ability to focus.

Entrepreneurs gain focus through experience. Everyone grows as he or she gathers experiences, but few people assemble their experiences into a system by which they can visualize end goals, seek funding, and attract talent to achieve something significant or build an enterprise. Experiences are the grit that grinds entrepreneurial lenses.

A well-focused lens doesn't make everything sharp. It doesn't see beyond its periphery. Foreground and background objects may not be well defined. But the objective and all the important objects that surround it are. This is where entrepreneurial focus is found. When the lens of the entrepreneur's mind finds the right depth of field, it sees everything important to the picture and little more.

Staying focused requires tuning out a lot of peripheral stuff. Distractions, unimportant side products, and an obsession with microscopic details will defocus or blur an entrepreneur's lens. Staying focused on creating a corporate culture that targets the company's mission becomes the CEO's primary goal. Most entrepreneurs achieve their focus by having their hearts set on accomplishing tasks that together support a visionary purpose. They see each task through before moving on to the next. Completion becomes a goal in and of itself because not completing even mundane tasks is the start of distraction from the mission. Entrepreneurs don't say to themselves, "I'm halfway through, so I can go work on this other project for a while." Follow-through is to them as important as getting started.

When I was first learning to be a pilot, my instructor told me to "pick a spot on the horizon and follow it; don't chase the instruments." Like a lot of new pilots, I would watch the craft's instruments and overcompensate for everything. The result was that I constantly fought the instruments; as turbulence causes an airplane to change direction, I would keep moving the stick to keep the craft's attitude indicator in the "correct" position.

"Don't do that," he would forcefully say. "Just focus on something out on the horizon. When you start flying IFR [instrument flight rules], then we'll teach you how to fly the airplane with instruments only." When you are flying a plane or running a business, if you chase the needle, you're not staying focused on the destination and you increase the likelihood of going off course or crashing. Chasing the needle is a game of reacting, not acting. Being able to focus on something out on the horizon, off in the distance, will keep you on track and not chasing needles. In every business, there is always enough turbulence to shake the craft, and so your gauges will inevitably bounce.

Focus entails knowing what to keep your attention on and how to respond. You will make course corrections, but ones that are focused on the end objective—the dot on the horizon—not a momentary jumping of a needle. You respond to market shifts, competitors' maneuvers, and new technologies but not to every minor accounting fluctuation or news item in your industry's trade press. Entrepreneurs make general course corrections to keep the airplane heading in the right direction.

Of all the things an entrepreneur should pay attention to, cash is king. More Silicon Valley start-ups have vanished through poor cash management than for any other cause, in no small part because the venture capital community makes entrepreneurs believe that cash is limitless. If you run out of cash, you run out of business. You have to be precise about how you manage cash.

Entrepreneurs often are not well educated about finance. Some don't even have a good grasp on their goes-in-tos and goes-out-tos. Entrepreneurs don't need to be CPAs, but understanding financials and understanding how your particular industry operates will give you a clear vision and view of how your business is performing and how your cash is securing your survival. If you don't look at your financials, you won't understand how your business is doing, and you can get off course in a hurry.

This is where knowing your business in financial terms becomes important yet tricky. Financials tell you about history but not about the future. Bookkeepers can tell you only about the past. A CEO needs to keep his eye on the horizon, which by its nature is in the future. Cash fluctuations do not make for financial trends, but enough of them moving in unison are like the stall horn in a plan: a warning that a fundamental problem is occurring. Cash management—cash flow, ratios, inventory cycles—is the alarm a CEO listens for while keeping her eye on the horizon. We'll dig deeper into cash management in Chapter 8.

Engineering fiscal safety systems—with financial alarms being just one of them—is one small yet important part of eliminating distracting clutter from an entrepreneur's focus. Maintaining focus is essential because starting a business and achieving the entrepreneur's vision are very much like eating an elephant, a process involving many small bites over an extended period. Since you cannot possibly eat an entire elephant in one sitting, you have to pace yourself and swallow what you can in phases, with the end goal being to ingest a pachyderm. Marathon runners I have talked to endure distraction in acute ways. Running long distances puts strains on the body that trigger natural psychological reactions. Around the 16-mile marker, even well-trained runners feel the body shout, "I have no more energy left." Yet a marathoner displaces even survival-oriented reactions to keep focused on the end goal. Marathoners and entrepreneurs have the unique ability to run on empty. When everybody else is throwing in the towel and giving up, the entrepreneur believes with all her heart, "I still got fuel to burn."

This is where entrepreneurial optimism and the viewpoint that obstacles are merely challenges come into play and focus the eyes of the organization. When the goal is long term—running a marathon, settling a continent, building a company—one must pace oneself, judge every obstacle, and determine how best to deal with it in terms of the long goal. Marathon runners don't quit when the road rises. American pioneers met tremendous obstacles as they crossed the plains and mountains of the West; they had no roads, they had few trails, and they had only crude equipment to bring their entire families over rough terrain. Entrepreneurs don't quit when there is a short-term sales drop. If an entrepreneur does not pace herself, challenges become barriers, and barriers obscure the goal.

In the technology industry, entrepreneurs are pioneers. When pioneers hit obstacles, they find ways around them. A frontiersman rarely said, "I've got a thousand miles to go," because that presented a huge psychological barrier. Instead, he would say to himself and his fellow pioneers, "I just want to make it to this next hill." Then, when he got to that hill, he said, "I've got to make it to the next valley."

Entrepreneurs operate in the same fashion, keeping the focus on a grand objective and dealing with every challenge as part of the puzzle of reaching the goal. Because of the entrepreneur's positive attitude and love of doing the things she doesn't love, the trip is as important as the destination. I don't know of an entrepreneur who doesn't have a positive outlook. Entrepreneurs don't look at the glass as half empty or half full. They see a glass that needs filling and go about wringing water from every boulder they encounter.

Part of their indefatigable drive is the learning process. Every obstacle is an opportunity to learn. In Silicon Valley, start-ups throw parties when they shut down, not bemoaning a failure but celebrating the thousands of things learned along the way. To an entrepreneur, adversity is manure; it stinks, but it helps her grow.

Although it might be nice to achieve success without obstacles, that is never an option, and without obstacles, we would never grow as people. It does take a certain amount of resistance for a person to grow, and entrepreneurs look at their very lives—not just their businesses—as a growth opportunity. Steve Jobs dabbled in the arts as well as technologies, and this drove much of the engineering that Apple created, delivering unparalleled artistic elegance as well as machines that shuffled electrons. If Jobs had not seen his own life as a journey of learning, the very nature of Apple would have been different and vastly less important, and personal computing today might still be driven by green screen terminals. Being an entrepreneur is running a marathon, not a sprint. Entrepreneurs may have to jog or even walk from time to time, but they always cover the entire 42.195 kilometers, not stopping at just 42. Entrepreneurialism is an endurance race that is made possible by focusing on the finish line.

FILTERS

Lenses rarely work alone. If you dug into the camera bag of any professional photographer in the predigital age, you would find a wide selection of lens filters used to change the scene the photographer was shooting. Today, digital photographers postprocess their works in Photoshop, which has an even better assortment of tools in an area of the application called filters.

Entrepreneurs must filter to maintain their vision. Entrepreneurial filters are designed to improve focus and clarity. Business offers an endless variety of distractions. Today it is an accounting anomaly. Tomorrow it is a competitor's product announcement. Next week it is an imperfect acquisition opportunity. Some distractions are obstacles, challenges to overcome in pursuit of the entrepreneur's vision. The rest merely defocus the entrepreneur, creating too many things with which to contend or spiraling his top management into analysis paralysis.

Every entrepreneur must invent her own filters that are properly fitted for her company, industry, market, and culture to maintain focus. Sticking to goal-related issues is hampered by suddenly shifting one's attention to things unrelated to a particular problem. Imagine being in your doctor's office, describing the shooting pains in your chest, but instead of listening to you, he is listening to what's going on in the lobby or answering an incoming call on his cell phone. By not paying attention to the goal—keeping the patient alive and well—he fails.

Both entrepreneurs and doctors can also become too focused, leading to poor diagnoses and improper treatments. It is a truism that surgeons like to cut; to a surgeon, every ailment looks like an operating room opportunity. Yet more holistic doctors make surgery a last option. An entrepreneur who is too focused can also ignore warning signs of internal problems or external market shifts that will destroy his company. Each entrepreneur must know the type, quality, and frequency of the information that is important to keeping his company healthy and then spend his time focusing on his vision. He needs to know what critical information to let in and what information to keep out because more information will cross his desk than he knows what to do with.

It is the scope and detail of information filtering that is daunting. At some point, filters become blinders. Too much information is like too much drag on an aircraft, slowing it down until it stalls. Too little information is like disconnecting the stall horn and not knowing you are about to crash. Oddly, entrepreneurial filters become blinders. A visionary leader can blind herself by using the same confidence that allows her to overcome all the obstacles thrown in her path.

An entrepreneur can become so convinced that the direction in which he is heading is right that he will ignore warning signs. He becomes myopic to the point that he is in effect not dealing with reality because some parts of the overall reality are not visible to him. If you put blinders on a horse, it won't be distracted by minor occurrences on either side of the road, but it also won't see the truck barreling down the side street. An entrepreneur who is absolutely convinced that the path straight ahead is assured is blind to internal and external changes that make a straight path a dangerous one. Keeping one's sights on the horizon—on one's goals—requires relying on the right data at the right time to eliminate the vertigo of self-assuredness.

John Kennedy, Jr., spun his plane into the ocean after succumbing to vertigo and not relying on accurate, timely information. He was flying IFR—under instrument controls—and was into some clouds when vertigo set in. His plane turned upside down, which made every maneuver he took the wrong one. Like every other aircraft, his had an attitude indicator. On these devices, half of the simulated horizon is blue and the other half is brown—blue is the sky, and brown is the earth. When Kennedy's plane got upside down, his attitude indicator would have shown him the situation. But he *thought* he was still right side up, and when he pulled the stick to cause the plane to climb, he actually pointed it into the drink.

Entrepreneurs get business vertigo when they fail to pay attention to critical and timely data, and push ahead with the confidence that they are still flying right side up. Early success is often a leading cause of overconfidence. Start-ups are notorious for basing long-term decisions on the success found with early adopters of their products. What worked in selling to adventurous, bleeding-edge buyers rarely works for the mainstream market. The entrepreneur boldly continues with the same go-to-market strategies despite the fact that his market fundamentally changes once he is selling to the market at large, the majority of buyers. The entrepreneur *thinks* his company is doing perfectly well when it is about to run out of early adopter customers and cash. He should have seen in his attitude indicator that he was looking at brown rather than blue.

In running a business, you have to believe your financials and your financial advisors. Numbers rarely lie and need to be held as sacred as the Bible. You cannot afford to think, "I'm going to ignore the warning signs when my inventories are going up and my revenue is going down." Financials tell a story, and unlike fictional stories, you must believe it. Financials are your IFR instruments. Disbelief in numbers and the trends they show is a key sign of entrepreneurial vertigo.

Conversely, you can experience vertigo by not having enough filters or the wrong types of filters. Having too few filters allows too much information into the entrepreneur's field of view, and this tends to defocus him. An entrepreneur can head off in multiple directions at once and cause the company to follow. Either form of vertigo is fatal to the company. The entrepreneur then needs to select the key indicators of his company and industry and limit his attention to them while remaining focused on the long-term goal. As with flying a plane, you keep your eyes on the horizon but frequently check your gauges.

In an airplane, there are six primary instruments (often called the instrument six-pack) which tell you different things: altitude, air speed, turn and bank, vertical speed, artificial horizon, and heading. Even in jumbo jets, these remain the essential instruments that pilots frequently check. Humans can safely fly with the birds because they have a small set of highly relevant and accurate pilot data. If a human had to cope with several dozen instruments, she would surely crash the plane.

Pilots constantly perform an instrument scan. Continual monitoring of the six primary instruments gives aviators sufficient information to assure that the plane stays in the air. If you relied on only one instrument, you might end up descending or climbing and stalling out. You have all those essential instruments because they back up one another.

I was flying my private plane back to the San Francisco Bay Area from my old home in El Centro, California. My flight path took me over the Tehachapi range near Los Angeles. I had switched my airplane to automatic pilot, and the craft kept its own three-axis controls as well as maintaining a prescribed altitude and heading. I was daydreaming and talking to my wife, flying under IFR (instrument flight rules) in the clouds. There was a strong headwind as we soared at 12,000 feet. It was all in all a very pleasant flight.

Until my stall horn sounded, telling me I was about to crash into the Tehachapi Mountains.

A stall horn will wake the dead and is designed to assure that the pilot knows the air speed has dropped to a dangerous velocity.

At first, this didn't make sense to me. The autopilot was doing its job; the plane *felt* as if it were performing correctly. But because I had started daydreaming, I had quit scanning my instruments and thus had not seen the creeping indicators that a dangerous situation was developing.

We were approaching the Tehachapi Mountains, and the nose of my airplane had begun to pitch up as my autopilot tried to maintain an altitude of 12,000 feet. Suddenly, my stall horn blared and woke me from my daydreaming. In this aircraft, the stall horns sound when the plane's air speed drops to 60 miles per hour. Now fully alert again, I noticed that we were losing altitude at the rate of 1,500 feet per minute—I was literally being sucked into the mountain by an extreme downdraft caused by the Tehachapi's Bernoulli effect.

The Bernoulli effect is caused by the V shape of the Tehachapi Mountains and the high-velocity winds coming from the north. The winds compress into the V-shaped slopes and create a vacuum on the back side of the mountain, the one I was approaching on autopilot. That vacuum was quite literally sucking me into the mountain. My air speed had dropped 100 miles per hour, and the autopilot compensated by lifting the nose of the airplane 20 degrees. We were a few hundred feet from crashing.

We were in panic mode. I immediately switched off the autopilot and pitched the nose of the airplane down. Los Angeles Flight Watch came on the radio because they noticed my ground speed had dropped to a mere 40 miles per hour and wanted to know if I was all right. "I'm a little busy right now. I'll get back to you," I replied. I was in the process of turning the plane a full 180 degrees and reversing my course.

As the eyes of the organization, entrepreneurs are constantly scanning the instruments—their discrete set of key indicators— but they also need to devise their own stall horns. Within every business and tailored to each industry, there is a collection of warning signals concerning the changing corporate status and market conditions, much like a pilot needing to know how much fuel remains in the airplane's tanks (internal conditions) and what the wind direction is (external conditions). You need this information constantly, you need it packaged in a rapidly understandable format, you have to understand the relationships between different metrics (as you would the relationship between air speed and altitude), and you need realistic markers of dangerous variations in the data to trigger your stall horns.

This is where top management choices are important. Good chief financial officers and chief operating officers should be auxiliary stall horns. They should understand the business impacts of changing situations and warn the CEO of dangerous trends. A CEO must maintain a relationship with these monitors of corporate health so that they can confidently burst into the CEO's office to discuss what they have discovered—they must be a stall horn that disrupts a CEO's daydreaming.

Yet stall horns are a last ditch device for averting disaster, and if your stall horns are blaring, you have not done your job as a pilot or an entrepreneur. Proper and perpetual scanning of your instruments is what keeps most planes from falling out of the sky and most businesses from collapsing. You are keeping your craft in its proper altitude and attitude. Consistently and constantly monitoring changing business conditions keeps your executive team on its toes but also unconcerned about having to perform emergency maneuvers.

Watching the gauges gives you an idea of the strength of your business. I look at Micrel's gauges every single day by reviewing the bookings, inventory levels, and changing customer demand. If it looks like bookings are increasing, I may let the inventory go up. If I see bookings are sliding, I can start ratcheting down inventories so that

I don't get caught sinking cash into products that are not moving. I examine receivables to see how collections are going. Watching collections tells me about cash flow and whether cash is coming in as it should. I also look at the quality reports, but on a weekly basis. I review them to see what customer returns look like so that I can know if Micrel has any legal exposure or quality issues. I look at the inventory's direction. I look at pricing changes. I look at factory utilization and also look at lead times. I meet weekly with my staff to go over business, and I dig into the sales numbers for each of the territories.

Those are the basic instrument scans that I run to make sure that Micrel's stall horns never sound.

Focus is essential and filters are important, but neither can be allowed to blind the entrepreneur. Scanning key indicators and allowing for important alerts keeps entrepreneurs from killing their own companies. Frankly, start-up CEOs are most often responsible for the deaths of their businesses and their dreams.

Perspective

Discuss nearly any topic with a San Francisco flower child and an Imperial Valley rancher and you will receive very different perspectives. The ways an entrepreneur views her life, her vision, and her company are all matters of perspective and ones she needs to constantly grow.

The dictionary tells us that perspective conveys the correct impression of height, width, depth, and position in relation to other things *when viewed from a particular point*. It is the relationship between aspects of the business, the market, and the time scale that defines entrepreneurial perspective. An entrepreneur knows two things with perfect clarity: the short term is used to achieve the long term, and he must view the business from every possible angle to truly see the relationship between the parts.

There are two very different schools of thought about how entrepreneurs view their vision and their companies. They either build corporations that last the ages or jump from project to project, starting with an exit strategy. The former is a business builder; the latter is a serial entrepreneur.

I won't denigrate serial entrepreneurs. They have their goals and their timelines. But when one runs a business for the short term without a longer-term view, one will achieve only a short-term result. Conversely, even when an entrepreneur has a long-term view of his business, he cannot forsake the short-term perspective. If he does not look at his business on a short-term basis, he can run out of cash and run the company into the ground.

The long-term entrepreneur has, I believe, a more integrated perspective on business, on people, and on life itself because she must balance the present and the distant future and create a corporate culture that nurtures people accordingly. She has a holistic perspective. Not only is this a greater intellectual challenge, it is vastly more satisfying. It requires building lifelong bonds and deep trust. It forces the CEO to think more deeply about the needs of her people and the future needs of her customers.

Indeed, balancing the long-term objective against short-term realities occupies a great deal of an entrepreneur's attention. When I was flying back to San Jose, the long-term mission of getting home was obvious. But my momentary lack of attention to the changing aeronautic conditions almost prevented my getting home, or doing anything else, ever again. The same thing applies to the long-term entrepreneur. Keeping his eyes on the bouncing gauges of his instrument board and on the horizon requires paying constant attention and constantly challenging his perspective. He has to quickly assess his options for short-term corrections that avoid disastrous outcomes yet keep his company's bearings. He must have the long-term view but review it on a short-term basis.

All that said, some entrepreneurs do take the short-term view with great success for themselves. They may have a five-year horizon at best, garnering venture capital and navigating to a profitable exit. As long as they can retire by age 45, they are perfectly happy.

But that does not create a lasting business. That does not protect all the people who helped make the entrepreneur rich. That does not dominate an industry or create a lasting product line. It may make a fair amount of money in a little time, but that is all, and since money does not equal happiness, it is of little real or lasting value. Bill Hewlett and Dave Packard did not sell out after creating an innovative audio oscillator in the 1930s. Steven Jobs kept innovating even after leaving and then rejoining Apple. Larry Ellison saw Oracle through the commoditization of operating systems and eventually the commoditization of database software, his original product line. They had long-term views and crafted companies to excel at achieving their entrepreneurial vision.

It is the long-term view that creates legends. A lasting business is one that can go through upturns and downturns over many business cycles. For a brief moment in history, Silicon Valley forgot those lessons and chased every short-term dream that a software engineer could devise. The dot-com era fallout shook the valley and the nation. The resulting recession made paupers out of paper millionaires. Everyone saw potential but quit treating business as a long-term endeavor. When signing bonuses for software engineers included leases on BMWs (yes, that actually happened during the dot-com boom and bust), one saw hundreds of companies take off like rockets and then crash like the poorly engineered vehicles they actually were. They lacked long-term perspective and thus never built long-term stability.

Building an enduring company requires having an enduring view of that business. An entrepreneur must want it to last forever, not just for the moment or even for her lifetime. Without this, there is an absence of perspective, which means the CEO lacks the correct impression of the relationship and position of all things. Most important, she lacks a perspective on people.

The CEO's perspective on people—employees, board members, vendors, stockholders—is ultimately important. Like a nation, a company is nothing more than people bound by a culture. In planning for the long term, corporate culture is as important as the people in the company, because it is what binds them and focuses them on the same long-term goals. Short-term entrepreneurs can build a culture, but it is certainly fragile and very likely to be focused only on money and shares. The long-term perspective requires sculpting an enduring and principle-based culture. This in turn requires a long-term, deeper understanding of people.

A solid corporate culture takes time—a minimum of 10 years. In a company's early years, there tends to be a good deal of employee turnover, too many issues, and too many cycles, all of which delay a culture in taking root. Anyone with a five-year horizon lacks the luxury of time to create an enduring culture and all too often must resort to bribery.

Systems built on short-term, money-motivated outcomes are inherently unstable. This is part of the problem with crashing start-ups and the darker side of the Silicon Valley culture to which venture capitalists contribute (as an industry, VCs are happy with a 1-in-10 payback on their investments; this exposes their lack of desire to create lasting empires). The pursuit of fast exits encourages short-term thinking, which encourages shortcuts: dangerous financing, low-quality products, sketchy customer support, and no corporate culture to speak of.

The short-term mindset is inherently broken; it is a planned obsolescence of the organization and the people in it. We refer to modern society as impatient and disposable because we want everything now—we don't want to have to wait. With instant gratification comes fragility of purpose. In contrast, tenacity creates longevity in business and in life. You cannot run a marathon without tenacity. Micrel would not have lasted since I founded it in the 1970s without tenacity. No marriage survives without the tenacity of the long view (I am now entering my fifty-fourth year of matrimony to the same wonderful woman). Silicon Valley entrepreneurs have a reputation for short-lived marriages as well as short-lived companies.

Like marriages, companies should be viewed as enduring, having a forever basis. I set the culture in place for my family to have an enduring marriage because I didn't want just a sex partner or somebody to cook my food or make my bed. I viewed my wife as my forever partner. I built Micrel with the same intentions and crafted a corporate culture with a forever basis in mind. The traditional Silicon Valley thinking claims that an entrepreneur sees a market opportunity and capitalizes on it. In reality entrepreneurs see everything differently. They see relationships, markets, opportunities, and life situations through a different lens than the rest of the world uses. They see enduring meaning, not temporary convenience.

It is the intersection of focus, filters, and long-term perspective that leads an entrepreneur to understand the value and mechanics of corporate culture; we will discuss this in greater detail in Chapter 5. Creating a lasting corporate culture cannot happen without the entrepreneur maintaining the long-term view and nurturing the focus, filters, and perspective necessary for continuous effort. Serial entrepreneurs are missing the perspective required to even start creating enduring cultures. Without the long-term perspective, they will treat people as a means to a short-term end, which is typically financial in nature. With this mindset—one in which people are little more than tools—culture is secondary at best. They and their companies look like fireworks: they shoot up, they look great and wonderful, they make everyone gasp, but then they fizzle out. People do not let out a gasp when they see a hoist lifting staggering loads onto an assembly line decade after decade, but they benefit from the endless stream of high-quality and affordable trucks and cars that come off that assembly line.

Entrepreneurs with long-term perspectives are hoists. They don't fizzle out.

INTUITION

Intuition is perceived to be second sight, clairvoyance, the supposed ability to perceive future or distant events. It is a word tossed about too casually in Silicon Valley, as though we manufacture mediums, not microchips.

Entrepreneurial intuition does exist, but it isn't magical. It is driven by the relentless observation of everything. It is how I came to conceive of a product that is now a standard part of the silicon chip–making industry and sell it to Texas Instruments before I ever wrote an engineering specification for it. It also led me to start Micrel because the entrepreneurial drive made me an ill-fitting cog in the machinery of slower-thinking companies.

I conceptualized a machine called the wafer stepper. Without going into the technical details, it was an intuitive evolution in the way the microchip industry uses light to create the semiconductors in everything from a refrigerator to an iPhone. Without the wafer stepper, shrinking transistors to their current size might not have been possible or practical. At the time, silicon etching technology allowed for accuracies of around 1 micron, or one-millionth of a meter, wide. Today the state of the art in mass-manufactured chips is 14 nanometers, almost 0.00000001 of a meter, or 100,000,000 times smaller than the standard of the time when I conceptualized the technology that has brought us to today's ever-shrinking silicon footprint.

The old process was based on using light to create photomasks: templates that filtered light during the etching of silicon wafers to create millions of transistors on a small piece of silicon. I got the idea not to use photomask-making equipment to create these masks but to image the transistors directly onto the wafer and eliminate mask making altogether. The benefits were enormous. The density of transistors could be radically increased, and the technique could easily be adapted to different wafer sizes. Accuracy and chip quality would also improve.

The problem was that it didn't exist outside my mind, and in that era nobody would want it because there was room to shrink chips by using the prevailing technology. But years later, when Apple put a computer many times more powerful than the Space Shuttle's onboard flight computers into your pocket, wafer steppers would be essential.

When I dreamed up the wafer stepper, the company I worked for was in bed with IBM, pushing a chip-making technology called e-beam, short for electron beam. Ours was a small company and had to ride this big horse while it could; there were no spare resources for new concepts developed by a salesman, which I was at that time. So the concept stayed in my head as I was sent to make Texas Instruments (TI), one of the enduring global chip leaders, a customer.

I was not immediately successful. I was turned away once. On a second try at introducing myself to a key TI contact, I was physically ejected from the building—tossed to the curb by two strong fellows, ripping my pants upon landing. My boss was encouraging in the old Theory X style of management, letting me know that failure to get the TI account was an employment-limiting prospect. "Any good sales guy will find a way to get in" was his lightly veiled ultimatum.

But TI was not interested in our regular photomask equipment, instead buying its gear from other, larger vendors. After my second attempt, my boss said, "You got to go back. It's important we get in there. You got to make some inroads." I couldn't think of any way to do that, but I had been thinking a lot about my wafer stepper idea and how it could in theory improve chip geometries. In those seemingly ancient days, the wafer stepper idea could shrink geometries down to 435 nanometers (0.435 micron), or about a third of what traditional photomasks could manage. Most people, though, would have asked why anyone would create a circuit for 435 nanometers if you needed it only for 1.5 microns. It was a technology to create devices nobody yet needed.

But I had a hunch that TI was already thinking beyond the limitations of current state-of-the-art wafer etching equipment, and so I devised a scheme to at least get a fair hearing for our traditional gear and then insert the wafer stepper concept into TI's collective engineering mind.

The third time I went to Texas, the receptionist asked me who I wanted to see and who I was. "Tell him his brother is out here," I told the receptionist, and then sat on the waiting room sofa. After a brief moment, I saw my soon-to-be customer coming down the stairs. He looked around for his brother and, not seeing him anywhere, asked the receptionist. She pointed at me, and when he glanced in my direction, I put a Cheshire grin on my face. He stormed over, obviously madder than it is safe for any Texan to be. "How dare you tell the receptionist that my brother is here to see me?"

"Well, aren't we all brothers and sisters in some way?" I said in the friendliest tone I could manage. He broke down and started laughing loudly. He picked me up by the arm and said, "Okay. Come on."

Once we were in his office, I started talking about the stepper. Keep in mind that at this stage of the game, the stepper existed only in my head. My company didn't know about this, and there were no specifications, no engineering plans, no cost estimates . . . *nothing*. I wasn't even expecting this engineering manager at TI to want the stepper. I just wanted him to believe that we were thinking long-term and thus that buying our existing equipment and building a relationship with us was a good idea.

But he was interested in the wafer stepper and called a couple of other people in to hear my story. I was very convincing about the nonexistent device because I thought it was a great idea but mainly because I needed TI as a customer. I did a little dog and pony show, making diagrams on the fly while telling them that the vaporous equipment was top-secret and that Texas Instruments was very lucky to be hearing about it so early. I certainly did not want them to go back to my company and tell them anything about wafer stepper equipment because it didn't exist and it was contrary to our being embedded with IBM on the e-beam technology.

The problem was that Texas Instruments was interested. They understood the benefits of the wafer stepper concept, saw value in it, and thus didn't want to discuss our actual, existing, purchasable equipment. They simply would not stop pushing me for details about wafer steppers. They disclosed that they had plans to shoot for half-micron chips because they were actively manufacturing microwave transistors and needed wafer stepper–level optical capabilities. The more I tried to discuss equipment I could actually sell to them, the more they wanted to discuss equipment that existed nowhere.

I went back home and never uttered a word about the wafer stepper except to my boss, who would want details about my foray into TI. Indeed, he specifically wanted to know if Texas Instruments was going to order any equipment, and so I said without a lot of confidence, "They're thinking about it. I gave them some literature, and they're going to get back to me."

Meanwhile, word of my wafer stepper idea circulated beyond my manager's office. Of course nobody else in the company had any idea what a wafer stepper was, so they called me. "Oh, it's an idea I was just telling TI about," I told them, and so my management did not take any action on corresponding with TI since they were focused on our IBM relationship and their e-beam technologies. Back office communications quickly died down, as I had hoped, and I didn't think more about it.

But TI did get back to me, wanting not to place an order for equipment we made but to ask when they could expect a quote for wafer steppers. I asked, "Well, how about my other equipment? Is there any way we can talk about that?" They were marginally willing to discuss our existing gear but again pushed for a quote on the wafer stepper.

This put me in a bit of a bind. How does one create a quote for something that their own engineering department had never spent a moment pondering, much less designing and building? I couldn't let TI go. Getting them a quote for wafer steppers was key to getting them to buy our existing products. Therefore, I decided to highball Texas Instruments. I fetched some quotation paper and typed up a quote on my own. Given the radically new capabilities of the equipment we had yet to invent, I decided that a price 10 times the going rate would be high enough to make TI blanch. At $800,000 a unit, even TI would not put such equipment into production, for it would cripple their profitability.

Never underestimate Texans or the power of market momentum.

They didn't blink. Not only was the $800,000 price not too high for them, they wanted four machines at that price, for a purchase of more than 3 million bucks, which was huge in the era of 1-micron semiconductors. The purchase order arrived with an urgent request for a delivery date for equipment my company didn't even know about.

My big mistake—though in the long run it wasn't a mistake at all—was to actually create a quote. Once issued, the purchase order bordered on an agreement. This put my and my company's reputation in jeopardy. Soon Texas Instruments was calling my company's headquarters, wanting to know about the status of its order. Soon my phone was ringing: "These Texans are asking about something we have never heard about." I rattled off some specifications over the phone. The somewhat bewildered voice from HQ said, "This hasn't been seen by engineering!"

Creating specifications on the fly didn't work, and soon enough things got so out of hand that my boss finally called me down to the Woodland Hills home office. "What is this wafer stepper issue that TI keeps calling us about?" I gave him the background on the idea. "Well, that is not a trivial thing," he complained. I told him that TI would pay $800,000 for such a machine, and that got my boss's attention. "Oh! That's not bad. But given the up-front engineering work, I wouldn't even consider doing this unless we got an order for five."

I reached into my coat pocket and pulled out the Texas Instruments purchase order. "Would you accept four?" I think he quit breathing for a minute or two.

We accepted the order and started designing the machine. This required diverting resources from our e-beam project with IBM. But if TI was eager to buy four borderline fictitious wafer steppers at

$800,000 a pop, maybe IBM would be interested in the technology as well. We sent the TI quotation and specs to IBM.

IBM's vice president of research wrote us back a stinging letter saying that the wafer stepper was the dumbest idea ever voiced in the entire chip-making industry (keep in mind that it is now the de facto method for etching chips). This was a huge problem since IBM was our biggest and most important customer. My boss tossed IBM's letter across the desk to me, and after reading it, I turned pale white. IBM's head of R&D was the most important industry scientist at the time, our company was insignificant, and the wafer stepper was little more than notepad scribbles.

"You really shouldn't work for anybody else," was how my boss summarized the fiasco/opportunity my wafer stepper idea created. "You just don't fit in. You're not the kind of personality that belongs in an organization. You really have to work for yourself." It was an invitation to "pursue other endeavors." It would be six years later that Tom Peters would write in his book *In Search of Excellence*, "If you're not getting fired, you're just not trying hard enough." I certainly had tried hard enough, and I did get fired so to speak. We both agreed it was time for me to leave.

I was walking up the stairs from the garage to my house. My wife met me at the stairs, as she normally does. "I've quit my job," I announced. "I'm no longer going to work for anybody. I'm just going to work for myself." It was 1976, a year when the nation was experiencing stagflation and economic uncertainty abounded. "Oh, okay," was her reassuring reply. "What are you going to do?"

"I don't know. I'll figure it out." And with that bit of confidence, I collected my last paycheck. I brought Micrel Corporation to life two and a half years later, in November 1978. It took a few steps in between because I didn't have any idea what I was going to do other than that I knew I was not working for anybody else.

Funny thing, though. E-beam etching technology basically doesn't exist today, and the wafer stepper is one of the most important pieces of equipment in our industry. The brilliant IBM vice president of R&D was simply wrong, being so thoroughly wed to e-beam that he could not accept a different approach. Like most innovations, the wafer stepper started with a bit of informed convergence, which is the essence of entrepreneurial intuition: seeing enough of the pieces of a puzzle that you suddenly see how the puzzle can be pieced together. Steven Jobs understood calligraphy and computers and saw ways to make one do the other. I saw how existing photomasks were limiting transistor shrinkage but how the basic photographic setup could be simplified to increase chip density.

Intuition is related to wisdom. Wisdom is the proper application of knowledge. We all gain knowledge, but if you lack wisdom, it means you will fail to see how to apply that knowledge for the improvement of anything, whether chip design or humankind.

First of all, you have to be wise—you have to use your knowledge properly. Wisdom comes through experience. The old truism is that good judgment comes from making mistakes, which comes from bad judgment. Thus, gaining experience should lead to greater wisdom. This is why Silicon Valley and entrepreneurs thrive on geekish exploration of anything that interests them: knowledge leads them to greater wisdom as well as great innovation through the intuition of applied wisdom. Conversely, if you are not learning through your experiences, you're not going to become wise and innovative intuition will not be yours.

One trait of wise people is that they avoid making the same mistake over and over. Their seeming intuition comes from accepting what doesn't work and continuing to explore what does. Learning from your mistakes and applying that knowledge productively is an ante toward wisdom. It is not being like God, for humans don't make perfect decisions. It all comes down to how we learn from our poor choices.

True entrepreneurs channel their accumulation of experiences—good and bad—and reduce their decision time to a fraction of what other people need, and often with less research. Why? Having learned from their mistakes, they see paths that offer low probabilities of success and are ready to try less explored alternatives. They make these decisions quickly because their increasing wisdom, along with knowledge and experience, creates educated gut reactions. A growing body of scientific evidence shows that physical responses felt in the midsection involve complex communications between the brain and the body; gut reactions are very real responses to stimuli. An entrepreneur stuffed with knowledge, experience, and wisdom has keen gut-level reactions and the confidence to make decisions that are based on them.

The ability to use all your experience, your knowledge, and your wisdom appears from the outside to be inspiration and intuition. Distilled, however, it is really well-informed decisions that don't require extensive, deeply researched, and group-based analysis (and the associated group paralysis). These gut decisions are fast and surprisingly accurate.

An old adage reminds us that there is a time for preparation, but when it comes to making a decision, your preparation is over. Learning is preparation. Doing and failing is preparation. Acquiring wisdom is preparation. All these things lead to making intuitive decisions, though there remains one vital element: principles.

Principles are fundamental, primary general laws and truths that lead to a specific basis of conduct or management. Closely related to ethics and morals, these are the optics of wisdom, guidelines that lead behavior by deciding in advance what is proper or improper. Without principles, civilization as we benefit from it today would never have developed. Whether it is Moses's commandments or the tenets of the HP Way, principles guide personal and organization decisions and are allegedly based on time-tested wisdom.

Culture, including the corporate variety, begins with principles.

Bill Hewlett and Dave Packard told their employees to conduct business with uncompromising integrity. Google's Sergey Brin and Larry Page preach not being evil. Both are examples of principles applied to corporate culture, which in turn directs decisions at every level of the organization. It is the process of instilling fundamental wisdom from top to bottom in a company. It is helping every employee make fast gut-level decisions without omniscient knowledge.

Sadly, many start-ups' mission statements are hobbled attempts at creating guidelines without principles. If the goal is to guide the decision-making process of all employees, the guidelines in mission statements must plainly expose organizational principles (often the entrepreneur's). This is where money-motivated entrepreneurs tend to fail, for they go to market without guiding principles and thus cannot enculturate their employees.

Principles can be visualized as a sieve in which each hole is an encouraged code. As any decision is made at any level, it must pass through each of the openings in the sieve. A company without published principles creates an environment where any poisonous element can pass, whether it is shoddy quality, misleading marketing, or financial fraud. Without guiding principles, the eventual accumulation of minor transgressions will kill the company. With principles—informed by the entrepreneur's knowledge and wisdom—decisions are made well and quickly, and the company thrives. Entrepreneurs need to add the discipline of establishing and publishing principles to their agenda and then live up to those principles by teaching by example.

Since nobody can achieve 100 percent accuracy in decision making, the entrepreneur must accept mistakes—his, his employees', his company's—as learning experiences that add to organizational wisdom and steadily improve overall decision making. One reason individuals and companies as a whole need to continuously experiment, try, and fail is that some knowledge has to be unlearned. Things change: technology, laws, markets, customers. With change comes the trap in which personal and organizational knowledge can become incorrect (principles are less susceptible, but they too may require modification over time). An organization in which failure is not tolerated is an organization that will eventually fail. Once organizational learning stops, so do progress and profits.

Principles. Wisdom. Knowledge. These factors can defeat gravity, cure disease, and guide the affairs of humankind. They even let a legally blind man take a company through an IPO and successfully lead it for decades.

When my second episode of retinal vein occlusion occurred mere months before the Micrel IPO, it wasn't clear to my board of directors and the people who were helping to take Micrel public that I could continue to run the company. My eyesight loss was dramatic and rapid. One day I had no limitations, and the next I could not read a memo.

It was a devastating moment. I, our employees, our board, and our financial advisors had labored a long time to take Micrel public. On the verge of triumph, the thought of reversing direction, of canceling the IPO and even searching for a new CEO, was traumatic. Making matters worse was the pressure to make a decision fast. People in the company and in the investment community would want to see corporate stability whether with the old CEO or with a new one. My impaired vision created one set of worries, and for Micrel to have a new CEO days before our initial public offering created a different set of concerns.

I had 48 hours to respond. In the meantime, my eyes were continuing to deteriorate. The inflammation was getting worse. My eyesight was getting worse. The doctors' prognosis was getting worse. My darkest hours were literally when my eyesight was rapidly fading, and Micrel's future was in the balance.

I talked to my wife and some friends. Being a religious person, I prayed for guidance. All the conventional thinking said I should call it quits and put Micrel into new hands. But the wisdom of knowledge, experience, and principle told me otherwise. I decided my eyesight was not going to limit me or the company. I made the decision to stay onboard and lead Micrel through the IPO despite doctors dashing my hopes of the condition reversing itself.

We went ahead with the IPO though I was working only part time; my medical treatments were interrupting the normal flow of work. My doctors were trying many things, from laser treatments to medications. It took a few months before my eyesight improved to even a marginal level, to a point where I could function acceptably day in and day out. During those months of treatments and rehabilitation, I started relying on different senses and functions. My memory improved considerably, allowing me to memorize nearly everything; that is convenient when you have to deal with people and changing situations. My hearing got better, not necessarily in terms of frequency ranges but because I learned to listen better, absorbing what people said, how they said it, and what they truly meant. I learned to listen intently because I had to.

I also became more empathetic. I became increasingly sensitive to people because I had to rely on others to get through a day. Perhaps I once had the narcissism of a typical successful businessman, but that faded when I realized how much other people helped me now and had helped me all along. I started recognizing that I was not an island, that I did rely on people, and that they relied on me.

I became a more kind, more gentle, more understanding person. Losing my eyesight caused me to see myself more realistically and to see others more compassionately.

I needed this challenge to help make me a better person. I let this challenge, this barrier, become an asset. I turned this minus into a plus.

But adapting took more than listening and becoming a better man. At first, I was in denial. I would think, "I'm going to get better, I'm not going to need help, my eyesight is going to come back in a few days." I remember waking up in the morning, grabbing my book, and stopping cold because my eyes could not read. Yet every morning I'd say to myself that a miracle was going to happen and my eyesight would return to normal. I even held on to my airplane for a year, believing in spite of the mounting evidence that my eyesight would come back. I held on to it almost as if it were a talisman, as if believing hard enough would make it all come true. After a year, though, I finally said, "It doesn't look like I'm going to get my eyesight back . . . ever," and sold the plane.

After a while, the harsh realities of my limited sight set like cement, and I knew I would have to make a new set of lifelong habits, to adapt to the new reality of being legally blind. I would have to function without my eyesight because that tomorrow, the one when things appeared clearer, when I could read my e-mail, when faces looked familiar . . . that tomorrow never came. Hope quit springing.

I found ways and tools that would help me adapt. This was long before the era of the iPad and personal computers that are helpful to the visually impaired. I started with simple magnifiers and bought glasses that were heavily bifocal. They didn't improve my eyesight to the point where I could drive a car, but at least they helped me see better. I asked my secretary to print the memorandums and letters I received in extremely large type so that I could read them with a magnifier. She still does this for me. Later, when iPads and similar technologies were ready, I found ways to enlarge type and have computers read my e-mail to me and transcribe my spoken words into replies.

Practicality confronts every entrepreneur. But entrepreneurs are not entirely practical people. It has been said that nothing is ever accomplished by a reasonable person, but more accurately, things happen when someone has the vision, adopts guiding principles, earns knowledge, develops wisdom, and applies it to get around barriers. Practicality is merely another obstacle turned into a challenge. People told me the practical thing to do in 1994 was to resign, to pass the leadership of Micrel to a fully sighted person. But I started Micrel with a vision, and what other people thought was the practical thing to do was not practical at all. It meant abandoning my company, my employees, my industry, my dream, my vision.

That all started in November 1994. Two decades later, my eyesight remains limited, but my vision has improved.

LESSONS

- Entrepreneurs' vision is not merely financial; it is holistic. Their vision is not through their eyes; it's through their minds.
- Focusing the organization on a vision is an entrepreneur's primary job.
- Staying focused requires creative filtering of distractions but also lenses to sharpen focus.
- Filters can become blinders when they prevent entrepreneurs from knowing the details.
- Obstacles are merely interesting challenges and learning opportunities for entrepreneurs.

- A course correction does not change the destination, just how you get there.
- Cash is king; keeping an organization focused on cash management is critical.
- Financial alarms are like stall horns in a plane, created to warn you about looming disaster early.
- Constantly scanning the instruments of the company keeps it from crashing.
- Details provide perspective, which makes the path and destination clear.
- True entrepreneurs build enduring companies that last and take care of their employees.
- Companies built on short-term, money-motivated outcomes are inherently unstable.
- Entrepreneurial "intuition" is the result of exploring outside of the box and seeing what can be done.
- Culture, including the corporate variety, begins with principles.

CHAPTER 3

The Heart

A newborn's heart is about the size of its hand, beating upward of 190 times per minute after birth. When the child reaches adulthood, the heart is still about the size of the hand, though now it beats at a more leisurely rate—about 70 beats per minute—because it has grown larger and stronger. In a day, the average adult heart beats 100,000 times and sends life-sustaining nutrition by pumping 2,000 gallons of blood over 60,000 miles of arteries and veins to feed the body's organs and tissues.

An amazing feat in light of the fact that an adult man's heart weighs only 10 ounces.

An entrepreneur is the heart of an organization, tasked with pushing his thoughts, vision, cash, and planning throughout the company. Like the human heart, he grows along with the organization, but that organism would surely die without its heart. Since the heart is the chamber of the soul, he also gives his dreams and passions to the corporate body. He is literally the lifeblood and life force of a business.

Micrel started as an infant with just myself and my cofounder, Warren Muller, (we could not have been more different—like a heart and a liver in the body). I was the heartbeat, setting the rhythm, the pulse of the company. It was apparent to me early on that rhythm in a company is as important as the heartbeat in a patient. A heart out of rhythm—quite literally in the condition known as arrhythmia—is a warning sign of death. An entrepreneur sets the pace of the company, changing the pulse as business conditions change and opportunities arise. He is the heart and a constantly running electrocardiogram report rolled into one.

Fortunately, most true entrepreneurs stay with their companies for a long time; otherwise the organization goes through a heart transplant, and those are rarely safe or graceful. In Silicon Valley, we see too many heart transplants in which the surgeons are venture capitalists. I'm not picking on VCs. Their business is earning a return on their investment in a specified amount of time. But since every organization has a pulse and since the heart of the organization has to grow along with the body of the organization, cutting out one heart and replacing it with a foreign one is traumatic and risks organ rejection in the form of employees not following the new leader (hence the benefit of careful succession planning and promoting from within). If an entrepreneur is not doing well enough fast enough, it is better to exercise her as one would exercise a heart and make it strong enough to help the body grow.

Organizational heart transplants are eventually necessary but are too common. The average life of a CEO is on the order of five to seven years. Hewlett-Packard went through multiple CEO heart transplants in just a few years, and little came of it aside from layoffs and growing employee dissatisfaction. Whereas HP once had a policy of promoting from within and had a series of sound CEOs after Bill and Dave stopped actively managing the company, it then started hiring CEOs from outside the company, and the entire HP culture— the HP Way—evaporated.

Putting a mismatched CEO into a healthy organization totally disrupts the company. It should be done only when the current heart is malfunctioning, when the coronary systems in an enterprise are clogged, weak, and beating irregularly. Sometimes a heart and a CEO are so weak that the brutality of a transplant is the only rational course of action.

Unfortunately, there is tendency in the tech industry to change the heart of a company on a regular basis, and it comes from being impatient. The board of directors becomes anxious about the way the company is progressing. Boards, especially boards with venture investors, are on a profit schedule tied to a return on investment (ROI) window. They want to ensure a certain return in a specific period. This leads to short-term thinking and the unnecessary surgery required to replace the CEO, often triggered by transient fluctuations in the business cycle or the shifting technology lead that competitors have.

Part of a new CEO's growth is how the entrepreneur becomes interconnected to the organization. A growing body of medical evidence shows the direct connection of organs within the body to one another and demonstrates how signals from parts of the body directly cause collateral changes. A heart is not different, able to receive data from the rest of the body and change its beats per minute and pumping force as needed. In return for monitoring and controlling blood flow, the heart grows stronger and more adaptive to change.

Along with providing nutrition to the body, the heart provides strength and feedback. The entrepreneur provides her employees with the same things, channeling them through the corporate veins: her personal interactions with every employee, the corporate culture, company policies, and the principles underpinning them all. At Micrel, we have four aspects to the culture of the company: honesty, integrity, the dignity of every individual, and doing whatever it takes with no excuses. When you strip human interactions of their typical failings, you find these attributes as the foundation of civilization and growth. When people—regardless of their goals—treat one another with honesty, have the integrity to deliver what they promise, never demean people or speak to them condescendingly, and then try their hardest, you bypass failure. It is the culture more than any other aspect of an organization that regulates the heartbeat.

Part of that culture communicates the passion, the soul of the entrepreneur. Like the passion one has for a mate or for creating art or exploring science, an entrepreneur by nature has a passion for the business, the industry, and the technology. A lack of passion equates to a lack of entrepreneurialism. Passion drives the desire to achieve, and a heart without passion desires little aside from existence. The entrepreneur—the heart of the organization—channels romance for his goal throughout his company and does so with an intensity that focuses others on a viable and noble goal.

That last part worried my grandmother. When I was only four years old she saw my drive, my determination, and told my mother, "God help us if Ray does not channel his drive and determination for good. For if he doesn't, woe be unto the world."

An entrepreneur's focus distills her passion through courage, vigilance, and resiliency. The world has many passionate people who lack focus. We meet them daily: good musicians who never escape the local circuit, talented painters still selling their art on the cheap at street festivals, and technical wizards with great inventions locked in their heads. Their passionate hearts are not channeled by a relentless focus, and thus their passion creates little outside their local sphere. The right combination of both passion and focus must exist for a person to become the heart of a company. Passion must be metered and directed toward the right objectives.

One aspect of entrepreneurial passion is that it doesn't die and sometimes doesn't even fade. Steven Jobs was innovating Apple products while fighting for his life. Larry Ellison ran Oracle into his seventies and then stayed on as a technical lead. Entrepreneurial passion is much like the commitment one has—or perhaps the commitment one *should* have—to marriage. The CEO must nurture it as he would the relationship he has with his wife. As time passes, if you don't nurture a marriage or the passion you have for your company, those unions will fall apart. Your eye can begin to wander, looking for a new mate or a new market. Perhaps this is the bane of the serial entrepreneur—forsaking a commitment for a fancy, wanting something new as opposed to building the family one already has.

I've been married for 54 years and have run Micrel for 37. Success in marriage and business has come from the belief that any partnership is not a 50–50 proposition but that each side is committed 100 percent. My wife and I never worry about unmet needs because we each try to provide 100 percent of what we need together. At Micrel, I could rest; the company does well, and I could work half as hard without immediate disaster. But committing 100 percent is how strong families and companies grow. It removes worry from your partner and eliminates the notion that "half of that is yours and half of it is mine." If people worry about dividing up work or profit, they never hit the synergy that creates multiple dividends, whether it is love of a family, growth of a company, or return on shareholder investment.

An entrepreneurial CEO has to view her role as a 100 percent commitment. I never worry about what kind of life mate my wife is going to be; I worry about the kind of husband I'm going to be. Equally, I don't worry about what kinds of employees my staff members are; I worry about what kind of leader I am going to become. As the heart, the pulse, and the soul of an organization, the entrepreneur must worry about herself above all else, because what she is and how she is involved affect everybody else in the company. She should focus on what she needs to do to strengthen the organization as opposed to what somebody else is not doing in support of that mission.

When this happens, when an entrepreneur is fully invested in his employees, an odd thing occurs: the entrepreneur is nurtured in return. The feedback he receives from his employees, his customers, and the market gives him lift. It reenergizes his passion and renews his focus. Success in channeling his passion grows his passion, just as exercising the heart muscle grows the strength of the heart. His success becomes the company's success, which in turn attracts driven people who want to be part of that success. It eliminates problems and lowers obstacles. It is renewing.

It is also essential to you and your employees. If problems become too great, people get fatigued, lose focus, and choose not to deal with them. We lost several great entertainers and writers to suicide because their perceived problems became greater than their passions. They saw less success and perceived more failure, and so they pulled the plug. Full commitment and the courage to pursue your vision keep the passion alive and keep entrepreneurs optimistic by manufacturing success and not succumbing to failure.

Passion drives the entrepreneur, but this begs the question of where passion originates. Not everybody is born with it. Some people never develop any. Most develop it over time. When I observe Silicon Valley entrepreneurs, I see the intersection of two things that create entrepreneurial passion: success and perception of the possible.

Success in the context of what creates entrepreneurial passion does not mean huge business wins. It instead comes from entrepreneurs learning that they can overcome challenges. Imagine two equally average looking men seeing the same beautiful woman and wanting to get to know her. The only difference between these two men is that one was fortunate enough to have had an attractive high school sweetheart and the other wasn't. Only one of these two men will have the nerve to approach the beautiful woman because he believes romance with her might be possible. Learning to overcome obstacles, no matter how small they may be at first, is the path toward believing anything is possible. John Kennedy knew that landing men on the moon and bringing them safely home again would be incredibly difficult, but he inspired the engineers at NASA to believe it was possible, and that made it so.

The second half is seeing what is possible. Most inventions are incremental, "plus one" improvements to existing products. Those improvements are seen as possible mainly because of their simplicity. More complex, market-disrupting products are also first seen as mechanically possible. Everything that is happening on the web and next in the Internet of things is happening because enough well-understood technology exists that any end goal that can be expressed digitally can be achieved mechanically. Google's founders understood two things with great clarity: that Internet searches needed to be more relevant and that mass-scale database technologies had matured to the point at which analysis to create relevant associations on a global scale was mechanically possible.

It is the intersection of these elements—the belief that one can solve a series of problems and the vision to see what is possible—that is the seed of entrepreneurial passion. Seeing what can be done (vision) and knowing that it can be accomplished (confidence) give an entrepreneur the desire to try. Because people visualize opportunities from products and companies that don't yet exist, all entrepreneurial quests are about the future—about what is possible and hence what is new. Nobody today strives to make better rotary telephones.

When an entrepreneur has the vision and confidence to move forward, one of the first obstacles she encounters is kick-starting her company and building her organization (never confuse *company* and *organization* because there are a lot of disorganized companies). Risk is the obstacle she typically faces, and it is the one that kills many entrepreneurial careers. There's always an element of fear because of the unknown, and with any business venture, there are many possible outcomes, including some bad ones. Risk creates fear, and fear creates inaction. Franklin Roosevelt told a worried country that it had nothing to fear but fear itself. If we fear, we never move forward. We won't take the next step. Fear is probably the greatest inhibitor, as many politicians have learned. It isn't restricted to entrepreneurial efforts; fear has kept people from becoming doctors and athletes, police officers and lawyers. A lack of confidence limits one's passion. Fear exists to protect us, but sometimes it protects us too much. Entrepreneurs must overcome the natural tendency to be fearful.

The entrepreneur's first challenge—and this is a challenge to his heart, his passion—is overcoming fear. Most entrepreneurs get this far because they have mastered overcoming technical obstacles but perhaps not personal ones. They know they can design a rocket ship but fear putting their money into building it and seating live humans in it. That's where courage, vigilance, and commitment help the entrepreneur overcome fear. Once the cloud of fear evaporates, the light from his vision matures his passion.

The tough part is slapping the baby. I know they don't hold babies upside down and swat their butts these days, but for centuries doctors did just that. In starting a business, an entrepreneur is basically bringing the infant body alive, with her passion being the heart within the tiny company. To start a company, to launch a product, to risk money and the time of other people requires overcoming fear and then bringing it all to life. The sense of risk can be monumental, but entrepreneurs who have the confidence in themselves to solve the thousands of problems—small and large—that will come and stay focused on their vision have little or no fear and bring their child to life.

Part of creating a company is removing fear from the people one brings into it. When I started Micrel, I borrowed money from banks by using my own personal promises and commitments. My neck was on the line. What I and my wife had earned and saved—our bank accounts, our cars, our home—was all at risk. I was not embarrassed to let my employees know this. My belief that we could create a company, innovate a market, and succeed in business was communicated by my willingness to lose it all. I brought the Micrel baby to life with my house, cars, and stocks in play, and every Micrel employee believed we would succeed because of my confidence (and perhaps the fear of watching me go to ruin if we did not succeed). Their fear was removed, and together we then focused on our achievements.

Doing this was aided by *not* taking venture capital. Free money, as some in Silicon Valley like to view VC cash, is easy to squander and comes with so many strings that an entrepreneur soon looks more like a puppet than a person. In exchange for being freed from control by investors, the banks created a list of conditions by which I would manage Micrel, such as minimal profitability and strict cost management. Little did they know during the negotiations that these were my managerial intentions all along. Altogether, this allowed me to run Micrel as I envisioned and kept me from the constant distraction of being managed by venture capitalists.

If an entrepreneurial CEO is the heart of an organization, venture capitalists are pacemakers. A pacemaker is an external device for regulating heartbeat. It has the advantage of keeping a heart rate rock steady but lacks the ability to make a heart grow stronger. A pacemaker works by running wires directly to the heart. Disconnect the wires and the weak heart will flutter and fail. Venture capitalists can keep the heart of a start-up running, but the CEO remains forever under the control of the VC pacemaker and the way it is programmed (and VCs are programmed very differently). When you do not produce the returns VCs expect, they can quit being pacemakers and start being defibrillators, trying to artificially kick-start the heart of your company.

Defibrillating an otherwise healthy heart is unwise.

Autonomy means you don't have to have a pacemaker or a defibrillator. Your company's heart functions on its own, finding its own rhythms and changing its beat to fit changing organizational needs. An autonomous heart tends to be self-driven and self-perpetuating as opposed to relying on external stimuli to keep the company functioning. It is organic as opposed to artificial. It runs itself instead of being operated remotely. It lives on its own biofeedback, not on an external signal.

Venture capitalists are also similar to pacemakers in that they have a limited battery life. They have investment objectives, not visionary ones like the ones entrepreneurs have. Exceed its investment horizon—regardless of how sound your reasoning is—and a VC pacemaker quits when its batteries run out. If you don't hit their targets, they're liable to pull the plug. An autonomous company strengthens itself and its CEO, making it ever more autonomous. A dependent company will falter when the VC pacemaker is removed. The more autonomous you are and the less you rely on these external stimuli, the better chance you have of succeeding.

It is conventional thinking in Silicon Valley that entrepreneurs need to be passionate. This, however, is an incomplete perspective. The correct thinking is that they need to be highly disciplined and passionate individuals. In life, passion without self-control leads to dangerous behavior, whether it is rock climbing without checking your lines or indiscriminately sleeping with many partners.

VCs can provide some external discipline, but it is far less complete than what a CEO with self-restraint provides, and it tends to be narrowly focused on meeting investment objectives, not creating lasting enterprises.

A VC's limited external discipline also comes from its limited business perspective. Like physicians, VCs have a finite amount of knowledge about the body that is your company. They don't know how the body is exercised on a daily basis, what nutrition it receives, and all the specific symptoms that a deeply involved CEO knows. Their guidance is designed for the average company just as your family doctor tends to prescribe medicine for the statistically average patient. Because they have leverage, you are forced to take their medicine even if you are wary of the side effects.

This is not to berate the value of the guidance venture capitalists can provide. If you are not an experienced entrepreneur or lack the discipline necessary to guide your organization through the thousands of obstacles you will face, VCs are applicable pacemakers. But you will be stuck with whatever programming they have, and your corporate heartbeat will be whatever they demand even if the pace is too slow or too fast. If you can't operate autonomously, you will require external stimuli to keep your company alive. Before attending a single pitch event, ask yourself if it is better to be autonomous or if it is absolutely necessary to live with constant external stimuli. Since anyone can obtain the discipline necessary to direct her entrepreneurial passions, I would advise the latter.

One of the disciplines an entrepreneur needs to rapidly develop is transferring her mission, vision, and passion to the entire company. This is the basis of forming and perpetuating culture. Without it, no two parts of the company are heading for the same objective, no two parts demonstrate the same values that underpin the company, and nobody pulses with the same excitement that causes the entrepreneur to leap out of bed every morning, aching to face the new challenges that come forward. The entrepreneur instills enthusiasm in his people by the way he speaks with them, how kind he is with people, and how upbeat he is about opportunities for the company even when business conditions are rough. He is able to instill confidence in his people that the company will succeed in part because he has a humanistic nature: he shows interest in his employees, asks about their families, asks about their health, and authentically cares about them as individuals, not just another set of faces at a group function. In return they absorb the entrepreneur's vision because they become interested in the entrepreneur. They will ask questions without fear because they know the entrepreneur on a personal level and feel safe inquiring about everything from the business strategy to the CEO's children. When you show interest in your employees, they show interest in you, want to understand more, and want to share the ride toward your vision.

The entrepreneur does this by developing interrelated disciplines. He learns to walk around his company and engage every employee. He listens more than he speaks, and this informs the entrepreneur and makes the employee feel respected. He has a set of principles and reflects them in every interaction. He has a moral code that becomes part of the organization.

That last discipline—developing and instilling a moral code—causes some people's teeth to itch. Traditional Silicon Valley thinking is that morality plays little or no role in being successful and that calculated amorality in the name of profit is acceptable. The correct thinking is that true and total success requires high moral standards. Morality is merely the adherence to ethics, which in turn are shared values. The core is the values with which the entrepreneur and his employees comport themselves. Without knowing, sharing, and enforcing a core set of values, the company cannot have a moral code and thus will have an incomplete culture. An incomplete corporate culture inevitably leads to incomplete success because someone in the organization will eventually violate ethical standards, which can cause customers to abandon you or the authorities to arrest you. A corporate culture built on principled ethics perpetuates business ethics. It is easy to do the right thing when a cop or your boss is constantly looking over your shoulder, but it is even easier to do the wrong thing when they aren't. Since constant monitoring of employees is impractical and a sign of mistrust, you have to build an ethical corporate culture so that everybody does the right thing in every instance without monitoring and direction. Your employees need to learn to do what is right when nobody is watching.

The uncomfortable reality is that there is no difference between personal ethics and corporate ethics. Companies are composed of people, and unethical behavior by an individual or a group within a company is a reflection of those people and of the lack of moral guidance by the CEO. People may be able to behave one way at work and differently at home, but that is rare. Indeed, some of the most amoral people present themselves as morally superior, perhaps to mask their bad deeds or sense of self-loathing. Eliot Spitzer, the former attorney general for and governor of New York, moralistically lambasted perceived corporate ethical violations on Wall Street while soliciting prostitutes, naturally without his wife's knowledge. His public life was presented as ethical, but his personal life was anything but. The two always reflect each other. If your personal life does not comport with your business life and vice versa, you will not be successful as an enduring entrepreneur.

As action without thought creates chaos, knowledge without wisdom creates failure. *Wisdom,* like *morality,* is a word too seldom used in organizations because the common connotation is too narrow. Wisdom equates to sagacity, discernment, or insight. It is the ability to base decisions on experience. Corporate morality and ethics are based on experience. Logic then dictates that a corporate culture based on principles and collective ethics reflects a wise organization that has the ability to think and act utilizing knowledge, experience, understanding, and common sense.

Part of perpetuating corporate culture is the perpetuation of the entrepreneur's passion as well as the corporate culture. This begins with hiring. Many people have come to Micrel looking for a job but obviously lacked any drive of their own and did not embrace Micrel's passion. The odds of such a person catching fire, of becoming part of a self-perpetuating organization, is remote; an entrepreneur might not be able to make this person passionate.

Those are people you avoid hiring. They might arrive at your doorstep with great education, broad experience, a nice personality, and a well-crafted résumé, yet I would rather hire people with more passion and less experience. Employees with passion will gain experience—they will actively seek it—and maybe even invent the next great technology. A person with experience and no passion will not and will dampen the passion of everyone else in the company.

Because the entrepreneur is passionate and disciplined, he always runs the risk of making his organization passionate but without the same discipline. You want your people to be as autonomous as possible so that they can create and innovate. But since action without thought is chaos, the entrepreneur needs to infect his company with the passion to strive and the discipline not to operate anarchically. Ironically, the same tools he uses to communicate passion are the ones he uses to communicate organizational discipline. He is involved with every aspect of the company, engaging with every employee possible and building a culture that values orchestrated action.

Micrel has a Friday meeting at which we bring the operations staff together to talk about various issues. About 30 or 40 people attend, and the agenda is designed to assure that everybody is heard, that we understand one another's open issues. A great correlation takes place at these meetings, where our separate and mutual objectives are understood and problems are solved. Individually we all have the opportunity to present how we are doing, describe what obstacles we face, and explore how we could help one another. Part of Micrel's culture is to make our mission personal and the culture upbeat, and so we end the meeting by telling a life story: something about personal triumph. This keeps Micrel's corporate passion high.

Yet every company is more than just operations, and so once a quarter we have a communication meeting at which we make sure that everyone understands how the company is doing. Our overseas divisions, being in radically different time zones, receive a DVD of the communication meeting. As an involved CEO, I usually give the quarterly report and then take questions. Different departments will also talk about their business units, their various issues, and how their work is going. The goal is for every employee to understand how the company works across the board, what the current status is, and where the mutual challenges lie.

Employees actively embrace what they understand: clear objectives, ethical rules to live by, and examples of when this all leads to success. At our semiannual achievement awards event, we identify people who have accomplished great things, whether internal efficiencies or acquiring a new patent (in Micrel's lobby, we have a plaque for every patent we have been awarded, and I fear we may soon run out of wall space to present them all). We publicly acknowledge and reward significant achievers, and this confirms in every employee's mind that our mission is obtainable, that our culture is the right tool set to achieve those goals, and that every employee is part of the program. With this deeper connection, all the employees improve because they lose their fear, believe they can excel, and realize they might well be on stage at the next awards meeting. It has become a continuous feedback loop.

Passion and wisdom will drive many companies to modest success, but determination creates the strongest companies. An entrepreneur without determination is an oxymoron, and an entrepreneur who does not invigorate her company with determination will probably never achieve her vision. But like unbridled passion, unfocused determination is a short road to ruin. Being determined while being unfocused creates unprofitable work. Determination toward achieving the wrong goal produces the wrong results. An entrepreneur and her organization must have determination, but without wisdom and discipline, that determination will lead both the entrepreneur and the company astray.

Passion and determination are related but are not the same creature. Passion precedes determination; without passion, determination never manifests itself. Even when passion and determination arise, their focus—the corporate mission—must be clear and constant. Too often an enterprise replaces its CEO with an outsider who imports his passionate vision, which is not that of the company. Armed with passion and determination, he starts running in a direction different from the one in which the company has been heading. This rips the very fabric of the company and ultimately leads to a short term as CEO and devastated share prices.

Worse perhaps is when a board of directors selects a new CEO with the specific purpose of not making waves. They choose a nice person who then relies on the organization to continue its former success. In both cases, the CEO is not listening to the corporate body, not creating a feedback loop and guiding cultural growth. Such CEOs are like marathon runners who ignore critical signals coming from their bodies and end up like the original marathon runner, who died at the finish line. Their misguided determination or lack of passion obscures signals the corporate body sends to change what they are doing. An entrepreneur must always be sensitive to his organization as part of the discipline of being simultaneously wise, determined, and passionate, just as a passionate lover listens to her mate. Being passionate without listening to your organization alienates the people you should embrace most closely.

One form of misguided determination comes from a naked desire for growth. In the silicon chip industry, there was one CEO who had a messianic mission to reach a billion dollars in revenue. There was no possible way to organically grow his company to that level in the time frame he had in mind, and so he launched an acquisition spree that proved deadly. Because his passion and determination were based on money and prestige, not on creating a lasting enterprise, he lacked wisdom and discipline. His acquisitions were executed chaotically. The acquired companies were integrated poorly because they were on an acquisition schedule, not a culturally sensitive and wise one. The discipline to do it right—to do the tough things first—was erased by his determination to do it big. His company eventually could not absorb the acquired firms properly and as a result suffered financially. They lost money instead of reaching his billion-dollar goal. As things got worse, he was constantly fighting fires and the stock dropped precipitously. Instead of creating or acquiring great products and making the market love them, they became defocused on the goal they shared with customers.

Then the personal computer market—the one in which his company had excelled—started to slide. Cash was thin from the acquisitions and the acquired technologies had not been properly integrated, and so they were not producing revenue. Had personal computers (PCs) remained a strong market, he might have survived long enough to sloppily incorporate the acquired companies, though it is doubtful he would have reached his billion-dollar goal at all, much less in the time frame he had envisioned. His misdirected determination caused the company's share price to drop by half, and it still hasn't recovered.

As you might guess, the board of directors performed a heart transplant and he is no longer running that company.

Other companies have gone the same route but have recovered their sense of mission and saved themselves from disaster. Cisco is one such company. After dominating its original markets in networking, it started an acquisition spree that puzzled people. At one point Cisco was in the business of selling portable video recorders to consumers, which is far afield from its core strength in industrial networking gear. This acquisition spree started to affect morale and earnings. But the CEO there did not allow his listening to be permanently impaired by the desire to grow. To his credit, he publicly claimed that Cisco had "disappointed our investors and we have confused our employees." They were able to manage themselves out of it. The CEO said Cisco would focus on five priorities and compete to win in its core competencies. Today the company remains quite viable.

Cisco is a strong company with strong leadership. With that strong heart, it survived a major mistake. As long as your company remains strong in heart, you can undergo a lot of trauma. If your heart's weak, the same trauma will kill you. Since the entrepreneurial CEO is the heart of her company, it is her personal strength that helps the company endure turmoil, market shifts, competitive threats, and the Great Recession. It can even bring a company back from the dead.

IBM had to perform a transplant, bringing in not only a new CEO from outside the company but one who had not led a high-tech enterprise. It was critical to bring in the right person because in the early 1990s, IBM was approaching bankruptcy. Previous CEOs had not listened to the market, and the corporate culture that had once thrived by placing all the effort into selling mainframe computers was forcing every activity to support that mission despite the market's active embrace of minicomputers, distributed computing, open standards software—everything IBM was not. A CEO is passionate not only for his vision, his corporate culture, and his mission but also to his customers. He listens to them as well as he listens to his staff. When customers—including those whose business he hasn't earned—speak loudly, a CEO's passion and determination must realistically bend. If the CEO doesn't bend, he must be replaced. But since such heart replacements are dangerous surgery, the new CEO must bring to the organization the correct new focus. Louis Gerstner rescued IBM from bankruptcy and stayed with the company for nine years, gradually shifting the culture to fit the new industry mission. Lou was the right choice for a heart donor. Leo Apotheker was at Hewlett-Packard for only one year because he launched an acquisition spree (resulting in an $8.8 billion write-down) that attempted to change HP overnight into a software vendor. Leo was the wrong heart donor.

Unbendable determination, being a trait of entrepreneurs, can lead to other problems. Some cross the line between being driven by a vision of their company and their industry and being driven by a vision about themselves. Ego replaces mission. Tiger Woods, Eliot Spitzer, Mike Lyon, and even Ray Rice have all fallen on that path. The divorce rate among CEOs and financially successful entrepreneurs exceeds the average because ego is crippling to relationships.

When their egos get in the way, CEOs become the business world equivalent of the rogue professional athlete. They view themselves as invincible and not needing to answer to anyone. They expand their personal risk, and to support their egos they increase their business exposure. When the media eventually catch wind of them being loose with corporate finances or women with whom they are not wed, it all comes apart quickly.

Humility is an essential human trait. An entrepreneurial CEO who works directly with all of his employees and who uses servant leadership remains humble. By focusing on his people to accomplish the corporate mission and by making himself their tool for completing their work, he avoids the tar pit of egotism. If your ego grows large, it interferes with every relationship, including your relationship with your employees.

Success can infect a CEO and swell her ego. Viewing herself as a success can lead her to believe that she is the primary cause of her company's fortune and thus that she can do no wrong. When you are cursed with a self-superior attitude, being a servant to your employees is impossible. Leading them toward a shared vision is impossible. Igniting their passion is impossible. All you can do at that point is scare your employees into cowardly obedience, which kills their passion, their determination, and their creativity.

Servant leadership is a very powerful means for developing entrepreneurial discipline as well as humility. To lead requires knowing why people follow, and you can never learn that without first following yourself. By being a servant to your employees—doing menial tasks from helping with funding a project to picking up a piece of scrap paper off the floor—you learn the art of following the needs of the organization and the people within it while simultaneously demonstrating a thorough commitment to doing what has to be done for the company. A soldier disdains the general who stays back at the Pentagon, but General George Patton's troops followed him willingly into battle because he was with them in the trenches. But you don't have to duck flying bullets to gain the respect and enthusiastic participation of your employees; you merely have to be involved as an equal and be willing to serve them. I have adjusted poorly hung pictures on the wall, served pancakes at company functions, and taken the time to talk to someone who lost a family member. By following, we lead and learn to lead. By serving, we learn to ask for service in the right ways.

Altruism is, or at least should be, part of corporate interaction. Corporations may not be people, but they are composed of people. They are not soulless abstractions. An entrepreneur who cares for her company must care for the employees as individuals. People uncared for become uncaring themselves. Employees treated as interchangeable parts will behave like machine cogs. But if the soul of a company lies in its people and is reflected in the corporate culture, the entrepreneur must have authentic compassion, understanding, and feelings for each employee as an individual. When an entrepreneur authentically cares about employees, they will in turn care about the entrepreneur, the company, and the vision.

The old saying goes, "If you worry about you, I won't." What this means is that when a person—in this case, the entrepreneur—is focused on himself, there is little reason for his employees to be concerned with him. People who are looking out for themselves, who are *looking out for number one*, eliminate concern from others. An entrepreneur who is obviously self-invested will find leading her employees difficult if not impossible. Such self-absorbed people, whether they are entrepreneurs or employees, are fairly easy to spot because they complain. They complain often, and it all relates to how their life is being made more difficult. They complain about their subordinates, they complain about the environment, they complain about their neighbors, they complain about everybody. Those individuals are often unhappy, selfish, and self-centered, and such people are prone to being swayed into unethical behaviors.

These are the people to not hire or to move to the front of the line should business conditions require layoffs.

These are all parts of instilling the entrepreneur's heart into the organization. With passion and confidence, big things can be done.

But they could be big disasters as well as big achievements. The missing element is discipline.

Confidence, passion, and discipline are in the soul of an entrepreneur and thus form the heart of the company. The entrepreneur is passionate about his vision, his industry, and his market objectives. He has the confidence earned by treating each obstacle as a solvable problem and a learning opportunity. He also develops the necessary discipline to focus passion and confidence on specific goals.

Discipline is the key to the proper relationship between confidence and passion. Passion involves doing the things you love, and discipline is doing things you don't love—or learning to love doing them—and doing them well. Discipline keeps CEOs and organizations channeled in the right direction. In nearly every instance, failed companies failed through a lack of discipline. Most typically they failed because the CEO was unable to control himself or to install organizationwide self-discipline.

The most difficult discipline an entrepreneur must learn is the discipline of listening for and accepting bad news. Every organization will eventually go off course. Sometimes they veer slightly as a result of minor internal issues. Other times they get turned completely around by enormous market shifts. His natural entrepreneurial passion and confidence can bring a CEO to disbelieve bad news and refuse to take smart actions. He has the discipline to keep his company on course for disaster but lacks the discipline to understand, process, and take action on bad news. In this case a CEO can also fail to recognize that he has become too cocksure and headstrong.

This is why being the strong heart of a company requires constant deep connection with all employees, servant leadership, and principled business ethics. The heart requires a feedback system. It needs information from the body to know when to beat faster and when to slow down. It relies on two-way communications through nerves and input from the adrenal glands. It is holistically interconnected to every organ, the marrow in the bones, and the oxygen from the lungs. The human heart would never function properly—could never feed the rest of the body—without constant input from the body itself.

The entrepreneur, the heart of the company, must be as deeply and thoroughly connected to the employees as the human heart is to the human body.

LESSONS

- An entrepreneur is the heart of an organization, pushing his thoughts, vision, cash, and planning throughout the company.
- Entrepreneurs need to transfer their mission, vision, and passion to the entire company.
- Discipline creates the proper relationship between confidence and passion.
- CEO heart transplants are traumatic to the company, and venture capitalists make poor heart surgeons.
- Entrepreneurs provide the corporate body with strength, nutrition, passion, and biofeedback.
- Authentic entrepreneurial passion doesn't die and sometimes doesn't even fade, but it must be nurtured.
- Entrepreneurs fully invested in their employees are nurtured in return.
- Employees actively embrace what they understand: clear objectives, ethical rules to live by, and examples of when this all leads to success.
- Entrepreneurs who connect with all the employees relieve them of fear and uncertainty.
- Servant leadership is a powerful means for developing entrepreneurial discipline as well as humility.

- Entrepreneurs have a moral code that becomes part of the organization; there is no difference between personal ethics and corporate ethics.
- An entrepreneur without determination is an oxymoron, and an entrepreneur who does not invigorate her company with determination probably will never achieve her vision.
- Overcoming challenges is a primary source of entrepreneurial passion; the other source is seeing the possible.
- Risk creates fear, and fear creates inaction. Entrepreneurs tend to be fearless.
- VC cash comes with so many strings attached that entrepreneurs soon look more like puppets than executives.
- Candidates who are looking out for themselves are the ones not to hire; they won't look out for other employees or the company.

CHAPTER 4

The Body

When I pumped out three one-armed push-ups, the financial reporter had no more questions.

I was in my early sixties, still at Micrel's helm despite lost eyesight and the seemingly endless suggestions that I stand down to pass leadership of the company to someone younger. The lingering suggestion was that I was past my sell-by date and was not robust enough to handle the rigors of managing a multinational, publicly traded enterprise. Most days I shrugged off the innuendos since they came from people unfamiliar with me or my self-discipline. They were simply unaware that in my sixties I was in better shape, more alert, and more deeply involved than entrepreneurs in their twenties.

Without help, I had traveled to the investors' event and given my presentations and was on my way to a meeting when this financial reporter approached me in a busy hallway. After a few predictable questions, she bluntly asked if I was soon going to retire and who my chosen successor might be. I could have explained my position, but that would have been just words, and in an age of political and business insincerity, words alone would not have been believed by her or by the investors who read her column.

Since actions speak loudly and images are riveting, I dropped to the floor in my tailored suit and my still buttoned jacket in front of whoever was passing by at that instant. I put one arm behind my back and pressed out three neatly timed one-armed push-ups. I jumped to my feet, wished her a good day, and went on to my next meeting.

Now in my late seventies, I am still fit and not immune to doing handstands for the fun of it. Being able to do physical stunts at an advanced age certainly shows discipline, but that wasn't what I was communicating to the financial reporter or anyone else. I was communicating to them and to everyone at Micrel that I was more than ready to continue running the company then and into the future.

It doesn't matter how able the mind is if the body doesn't listen. Stephen Hawking, the brilliant theoretical physicist at Cambridge, possesses one of the most amazing minds of any generation. But he also has a disease akin to amyotrophic lateral sclerosis (ALS), a disorder in which the motor neurons in the brain, brain stem, and spinal cord are dying. It does not matter what Professor Hawking says to his body: it doesn't hear him. His mind, which conceptualizes the invisible fabric of the universe, can also visualize walking, talking, and dancing. But the strength of his mind is useless in commanding his body because the paths of communication to his arms, legs, and jaw are disappearing from within.

We have established that the entrepreneur is the mind and the heart in his or her organization. But beyond the mind is the body: the hands on the assembly line, the arms in human resources, and the legs in the sales department. Without constant and clear communications to and from the brain, the body fails. It may last for a while on autonomic reflexes and collateral communication between its various parts, but it will invariably die.

At the age of 77, I can still do one-armed push-ups because I took the time to develop the strength, balance, and coordination and my body remembers how. I have a younger friend who tried doing a one-armed push-up and almost broke his nose when he hit the floor hard. He wasn't a weakling, so it wasn't a simple matter of strength. It also involves flexibility, coordination, and coaching the various body parts to act in harmony to achieve that goal. Coordinated moves within a company produce similar results, such as getting manufacturing to work with finance and both to coordinate with sales and marketing. When the members of each department actively learn about the other groups' jobs, they understand how their actions affect other departments and how other departments affect them.

When I dropped to the investor conference floor with my athletic demonstration, I was communicating as much to Micrel employees as I was to the reporter. That is a major part of an entrepreneur's job: communication. Entrepreneurs must communicate the mission, the values, the policies, and the market realities of the company. They are not pitchmen, because everybody eventually sees through a sales job or a snow job. They are the brain in the corporate body, pumping out relevant information to all the employees in ways that can be understood and embraced and that drive employee activities toward well-understood goals.

This perhaps is why agreement between the entrepreneurial mind and heart is absolutely essential. We have all met someone who says one thing and then seems to act as if she has a completely different plan. We spot them quickly enough in our adulthood. We have learned to watch for such people and distrust them. When an entrepreneur says to her employees that she wants to build a thriving enterprise that nurtures all the employees but seems motivated only by her incentive bonus and stock options, we assume she is a liar. A mismatched entrepreneurial heart and mind will be detected by employees as surely as a used car salesperson's assurance about how a car was owned by a grandmother who only drove to church on Sundays.

In a company with a conflicted heart and mind, the body cannot respond properly. It will not listen, cannot be trained, and will lack the discipline necessary to learn and grow. This is why short-range financial incentives and goals lead to floundering companies: the corporate body never matures. It never learns the routines or masters the skills necessary to achieve a long-term mission. Since all learning is incremental, even short-term wins do not lead to long-term success because the corporate body never makes the necessary serial, incremental improvements or incorporates their lessons.

Every gymnast knows the process. It takes years of training, educating every tissue from the largest strength-focused muscle to the tiniest balancing ligament. I used to marvel at people who could walk on their hands, wondering how they did it. The act isn't natural. I had to learn that stunt in increments, starting with basic handstands and building the strength to hold that position. Later I learned that to walk on your hands requires picking one hand up off the ground completely and thus balancing on just one hand. That took time to learn and caused muscles I wasn't aware I owned to hurt the next day. It also required teaching some parts of my lower body (my upper body in this position) to either help balance me or hold perfectly still. After the incremental learning of how to walk forward, I had to learn to walk backward. Then I had to apply all that knowledge to walking up a set of stairs, which again required my body to learn new ways to balance as one hand left the ground, landed on a higher plane, and then pushed the entire body upward.

I can still do that today. Bodies and corporations develop muscle memory and coordination to perform difficult tasks. The corporate mind has to be willing, but so too does the corporate body, and the mind leads the body in that direction, teaching it how to learn.

The theme here is harmony. A passionate heart and a thoughtful mind will not create a competition-worthy gymnast. Neither will a headstrong entrepreneur with a nifty idea create a viable enterprise. It took coordination to walk up steps on my hands, and it took the coordination of thousands of people inside and outside of our corporate headquarters to make Micrel a thriving enterprise. The head count is less important than the way employees work together, the way they are coordinated in reaching common goals. Micrel has a small head count yet performs with a profitable consistency that is unmatched in the industry and in most publicly traded companies. This is due not to entrepreneurial genius but to the willing coordination of everyone involved.

Entrepreneurs need to develop a great deal of skill and sensitivity to get many people working together well and consistently.

Imagine the junior MBAs Micrel occasionally hires. I want them to understand the financial structure of the company and how it works, but I also want them to understand R&D and the issues that department faces. I have to ensure that cross-pollination takes place so that each group understands the functions of the other group and appreciates its needs. Not that I want them to become experts in a particular area, but I want them to understand and be sensitive to how their decisions affect other parts of Micrel. I have all the departments meet once a week to coordinate their activities and understand one another's issues and needs.

For all of this, the entrepreneurial CEO must understand that she plays a role that lacks a certain amount of glory. Snipers, the most dreaded soldiers on the battlefield, are part of a two-person team whose other member is the spotter. Snipers depend on spotters to hit their targets. Spotters track the target, keep tabs on wind direction and speed, and watch for changes downrange, constantly relaying instructions to the sniper. A start-up CEO might like to think of himself as the sniper, targeting a market or industry. But in reality he is the spotter, gathering information and then coordinating the actions of the snipers in his company.

Coordination requires the body—the employees receiving coordinating instructions—to willingly act on them. A would-be gymnast will fall from a handstand if her body isn't prepared to follow instructions from her brain. Employees who don't understand the mission or trust the guidance of the CEO will do the same thing. Understanding people, the ways they learn, the ways they develop trust, and what makes them want to perform is a prerequisite to training the corporate body.

Oddly, the best place to start learning how to lead and communicate is outside a corporation.

As the oldest of 11 children, I was thrust into coordinating sibling activities for daily service to the rest of the family. Not owning a dishwasher, I learned how to organize the washing of dishes for 13 people three times a day. I have been active in my church, which is a very people-focused place and is highly organized. I also served as a member of the board of trustees for the Saratoga Elementary School, a role that presents the challenge of balancing the interest of teachers, parents, taxpayers, and administrators, all with the obvious mission of providing superior education to children.

None of these roles was focused on getting rich but required getting the voluntary participation of people without any financial incentives. Such extracurricular work teaches entrepreneurs much about human motivation, serving others as a prelude to leading them, and why trust is the cornerstone of their participation. Contrary to Silicon Valley sensibilities, I think would-be entrepreneurs would do well to spend a few years working at unprofitable or even philanthropic pursuits before starting a company. The education will make a person into a true leader.

It also teaches entrepreneurs about willfully giving of rather than taking for themselves, which becomes the foundation of servant leadership. Are you a giver, or are you a taker? Working for churches, nonprofit organizations, and school boards offers few taking opportunities, and so they make great training grounds for the art of giving your time, attention, and effort to other people. The people in such organizations reciprocate and give of themselves, which exposes another truth about cooperation in life and in organizations. You can give only as much love as you are willing to receive. If you do not accept help from others, you are less likely to get help. You have to be willing to let others help you, and that begins with showing gratitude for their help. Gratitude is cleansing and motivating, and soon enough it starts showing up throughout an organization.

We can't live as though we were on an island. We are surrounded by other people and have to be grateful for what they do in their functions whether it is your barber or the grocer or whoever you need to express appreciation for. That is the biggest challenge in our hectic lives. We can become unwilling to take the time to be grateful, to thank others for the job they do. We should give a person a tip, open the door for somebody, help a frail person cross the street, or stop and change the flat tire of a mom stuck on the freeway.

Gratitude is a discipline that entrepreneurs lack in general and that keeps them from coordinating the body of their organizations well. Young entrepreneurs in particular fail to express appreciation— to praise their people, to praise the organization even when it is doing poorly. It is easy to praise people, departments, divisions, and even entire companies when they do well, but that is when people are *already* motivated. When things are tough and times are hard, that is the time employees need your most sincere appreciation. Management studies have shown that employees appreciate praise more than anything else. Give employees a bonus check and they will be grateful, but the memory of that money lasts only a short while. Give them a plaque and 40 years from now they will know exactly where it is even if it is tucked away in a box in the basement and will tell the story of how they came to earn that recognition.

We see stories on the news from time to time that illustrate how the power of looking out for others—paying it forward—works miracles. Somebody will pull into a KFC or Starbucks drive-through and when placing an order will tell the cashier that he or she is paying for the person in the next car. It has a ripple effect. One such story had a person farther back in the line getting coffee and breakfast at no cost for everyone in his car pool as a result of the compounded appreciation shown by strangers. Appreciation, whether at a Starbucks drive-through or between an entrepreneur and the employees, snowballs. If you are truly appreciative for what someone else has done, that person will show the same appreciation to others. Similarly, you become more likely to show appreciation to the next person you encounter. Honest gratitude is a human trait that helps employees thrive.

So too is knowing that the entrepreneur takes risks and shares their pain. Like all companies, Micrel has on rare occasions needed to furlough employees. Not getting paid for a week or two can be tough on families, and so when these furloughs were necessary, I took twice the amount of unpaid time as my employees (though I still came to work each day). When we had to have salary cuts, if my team took a 5 percent hit, I took a 10 percent reduction. In Micrel's early days I made sure the employees understood that I had secured the equivalent of $900,000 in today's money in personal debt to launch the business and give them jobs. All too often CEOs find ways to shift pain and risk to their employees. The employees know this and respond accordingly by no longer caring if the entrepreneur, the CEO, or the company survives.

None of these steps is required legally or morally, but it keeps the faith with employees and multiplies trust. I always put myself at risk more than I put my employees at risk. I make sure that my stock compensation is at or below the midpoint of that of my peers. I have declined salary increases. I have declined stock options when the company was not doing as well as I wanted. I arrange my cash bonus incentive cliff so that if the company does not hit our goals, I receive nothing. That's always been the mantra of how I run Micrel: I do what I say I will or I don't get paid.

It has been my goal to ensure that as a leader I never ask something of my team that I am not willing to do myself and then do even more.

Yet no organization survives on emotions. Whenever two or more people collaborate on a mission, certain rules are established to maintain order. If you don't believe this, look at the accumulated rules you and your spouse have, starting with the ones outlined in your wedding vows. Every organization, no matter how small, has some regimentation. *Regimentation* is one of those unfortunate words that sound more callous than their definitions relate. Regimentation exists to create the disciplines necessary to ensure uniformity of action. It can be harsh, such as the regimentation instilled by a drill sergeant, or it can be kind, such as the comforting guidance provided by a schoolteacher. Each mode exists for the same purpose, however: to create some degree of uniformity.

Every company has regimentation, but for entrepreneurs, financial regimentation is essential. There are reasons for being financially regimented. The fact that Micrel has had only one unprofitable year since 1978 and has had very few cutbacks is proof that cash control regimentation has value.

Simple and sound financial regimentation goes against some venture capital theory and practice in Silicon Valley. Some VCs allow their portfolio companies to lose money for a while on the theory that building market share is sacred. They keep the lure of more money—follow-on rounds—in front of the entrepreneurs at all times, letting them focus on managing their market outreach rather than regimenting their finances. These follow-on rounds often deplete the entrepreneur's control of the company further and ultimately lead to her dismissal if profitability goals are not met.

The problem is that this establishes bad habits, and like cigarette smoking and hard drinking, those bad habits are hard to break. As with all other addictions, it is best not to start at all. You cannot become a heroin addict if you never fill a syringe, and you cannot become dependent on venture capital cash if you never offer a term sheet. Micrel never took venture capital despite the fact that it is plentiful in Silicon Valley and is considered essential in starting a microchip business. Yet we have been profitable from day one as a result of financial regimentation. Running Micrel that way not only has ensured profitability but also has created good cultural habits that avoid wasteful spending and encourage sound cash management throughout the organization.

Regimentation is not easy, especially for a new company and a first-time entrepreneur. It is one of the doing-tough-things-first actions an entrepreneur faces. It is at the very heart of an entrepreneur's tough actions because a company without cash doesn't live and managing cash becomes the first difficult and often unpleasant job. It is the one task that cannot be successfully delayed: procrastinating does not improve an organization's financial regimentation. It is difficult to be profitable from day 1 but doable, as Micrel demonstrated. It requires doing this one tough thing first: establishing the regimented principle that you can be profitable, that you can manage cash effectively, that every employee is part of a fiscal responsibility discipline, and that the company will not procrastinate in doing so. The consequences of thinking otherwise are too high.

Conversely, too much regimentation can be harmful. A company must grow, and being tightfisted in the wrong places can choke growth or alienate employees. If you put too many controls in place, you can create organizational paralysis. You need sufficient regimentation so that the company's health is not endangered but also need financial freedom of movement so that you can advance in your chosen markets. The constant question an entrepreneur asks is, "Does this spending help accomplish the mission and our vision for achieving that mission?" Most of the time, the answer is no.

Fiscal regimentation can also be called corporate *frugality*, another word with unfortunate connotations. Stripped of the inappropriate miserly association, frugality simply means a lack of wastefulness, which has inherent value in running a business. Every resource—corporate cash, clean water, forests—is limited. Most resources are renewable if managed properly. Treatment plants turn sewage into potable water. Replanting creates new forests. Non-wasteful spending makes money available for business cycle downturns and exciting new market acquisitions. Large families figure out the benefit of frugality early on, strategically handing down clothing, optimizing grocery shopping, and enjoying simple pleasures instead of elaborate entertainment.

When I started Micrel, I sought discarded equipment. In those early days it would have been wonderful to buy new manufacturing gear, but the price difference between new, state-of-the-art gear and what was used but otherwise viable was significant. We found previously owned equipment, refurbished it, and put it into production. As a side effect we developed a culture of corporate frugality that has lasted to this day. Capital expenditures need to be justified and show a realistic return on investment.

The inherent value of frugality to an entrepreneur is flexibility and agility. Nothing hamstrings an entrepreneur more than lacking the cash necessary to implement his vision and accomplish his mission. Wasting cash on anything that doesn't drive the organization toward the mission makes achieving the objective much more difficult, and that frustrates everyone in the company. Wasting money wastes people, market advantage, and opportunity. It wastes time and burns out employees.

I can tell when an entrepreneur is endangering her company with a lack of financial frugality. It first shows up in the lobby, which is more posh than even those of large and highly profitable multinational companies. It is a transparent attempt to look more successful than the company truly is. Next comes the company cars, which may be a functional necessity but not when luxury town cars are leased for salespeople. Next comes having the members of the management team fly first class when business or coach is more than adequate. Then there are the beautiful cafeterias with academy-trained chefs, free lunches (which we all know are never free in the long run), and more. A lack of frugality is a large-scale diversion of resources from the mission and shows that accomplishing the mission has become secondary.

It rarely lasts. Eventually two things happen in rapid succession. First, a cash flow crunch creates an urgent need to cut back expenses. Then the people most addicted to the luxuries provided by wasteful spending are the ones who complain the loudest, and that creates trickle-down dissatisfaction. Recall that gratitude paid forward generates as much or more in return. So does ingratitude. People are grateful for expensed automobiles and free food and can become ungrateful when those things are no longer viable. Yet if the same money had been spent on accomplishing the corporate mission, growing the company, and expanding employee job security, the bilateral gratitude would have grown as well.

Frugality starts with the entrepreneur. Ignoring politics, California's repeat governor Jerry Brown understood this when he first took office in the 1970s. He eschewed the governor's Cadillacs and drove around the state capital in an old Plymouth. He did not move into the governor's mansion, taking residence in much more modest digs. He realized that at that time—a period when state spending needed to be reduced—any ostentatious display on his part would create a public backlash. Entrepreneurial CEOs have the same effect on their employees whether in personal accoutrements or in lavish mahogany waiting room furniture.

A company I once worked for that no longer exists was addicted to wasteful spending, and when I did the opposite, nobody understood why. In current dollars, I and the other salespersons were given a $6,000 travel allowance. I turned in an expense report for less than $400. Whereas other salespersons took limousines to and from the airport, I drove myself or took a taxi. When they sought out a great steak house, I drove through McDonald's. There was no great advantage to wasting the company's money aside from my own personal pleasure, and so I chose not to.

I was told I could not submit that expense report because it would set the wrong example for the rest of the company. It remains unclear to me what example they were trying to set. Wasteful spending was a sign of disrespect to the company, which meant disrespect to everybody who labored there. Their hard work, their dedication, their hopes for a secure future would have been compromised, and I simply could not do that. I respected them too much.

To speak Silicon Valley heresy, I contend that it is mechanically impossible to be too frugal, because the outcome of excessive frugality is business failure and bankruptcy. There is a point in controlling spending where it begins to damage the company and thus lead it to a financial breakdown. If you don't pay your employees, if you don't have the proper benefits package, if you don't monitor the health of their livelihood, they will leave and wound your business. Employee turnover is a great indicator that you have become too frugal and thus uncompetitive. Employees are an investment, and they return to the company more than you put into them. Like any other resource, they are limited and sought after by your competitors. Employees, like manufacturing equipment, waiting room furniture, desktop computers, and other elements essential to running a business, are investments that are worthwhile but must be frugally acquired. Spend too little and you won't have employees. Spend too much and they may develop an addiction to excess.

As you grow, what was frugal becomes an impediment. I discovered this when Micrel became a thriving and important company.

The quality of a good board of directors cannot be overstated. The board helps the entrepreneur find her way through complex markets and equally complex internal management. In a company's early years, adequate board members are reasonably easy to come by and relatively inexpensive. But as a company grows and the stakes become larger, you need to acquire board members with more discipline, better track records, and keener insights. With greater growth comes greater risk to the company and to the directors should something bad happen.

Here is where my frugality caused problems. For years I fought against obtaining directors and officers liability insurance (D&O). This insurance is payable to the directors and officers of a company or to the company itself to cover losses or defense costs from legal actions, which have become more common. It seemed to me to be a wasteful expense given Micrel's impeccable track record and corporate culture of honesty and integrity. If I, my board, and my employees didn't do anything wrong, the insurance premiums were wasted cash. Yet each year it became more difficult to recruit board members because they insisted on the protection of D&O policies. At some point my frugality became an impediment to creating a great board of directors and thus became an impediment to Micrel.

We see, then, that frugality is part of training the corporate body and that not being obstinately frugal is part of feeding the business organism. In the hierarchy of conditioning the organization, after not wasting cash, hiring the right people, eliminating worry, and preserving resources, it is necessary to create the desire among all employees to participate. Success breeds success, which isn't much value to start-ups without track records. People respond to being appreciated and respected and being treated with fairness and given the necessary tools to accomplish the mission. In every organization, fairness, respect, and appreciation drive the members. Our armed services combine these ingredients in their treatment of soldiers, sailors, and marines and have no room for slack or discordance.

Trust, sadly, is hard to come by in these cynical times. Trust must always come from the very top, but in the modern era it is essential that trust in the entrepreneur be authentic and that it pass down through every level of the organization. If trust is violated at any management position, everyone in the chain of command can become reluctant to do his or her best. Studies have shown that the primary reason people leave a company is that they didn't like the supervisor, and most of the time that dislike arises from distrust. If the CEO is not trustworthy, the entire organization becomes infected with suspicion.

Similarly, if the employees believe the CEO truly understands and appreciates who they are, they go beyond working eight hours a day. They think, collaborate, explore, and find efficiencies. They participate as opposed to making a paycheck. They become fully integrated parts of the corporate body, responding to conditions, running toward the same goal as everyone else in the company. They catch the entrepreneur's fire, inherit his confidence, and achieve more than they thought they could. These factors combined express the employees' happiness, which in turn defines the happiness of customers, investors, and partners.

The king of Bhutan coined the phrase "gross national happiness" as part of a moral national philosophy that centered on the belief that money is subservient to happiness in people's lives. A common slogan in Bhutan these days is "Gross national happiness is more important than gross national product." From such a small country has sprung the very powerful idea that what is important to people is the pursuit of happiness. If money is less important than happiness, one of an entrepreneurial CEO's missions is the preservation and growth of his employees' happiness, acknowledging that money is a factor but not *the* factor. Having happy employees who believe they are a part of an organization that appreciates them affects other employees. They in turn affect the quality of products, interactions with customers, technical support experiences, and the bottom line.

Unhappy yet successful organizations are rare because this is an oxymoron. Unhappy employees leave, and the organization either ceases to exist or becomes populated with fear-inflicted staff. Liz Wiseman wrote eloquently about how good leaders are magnifiers, though what they magnify is important. A CEO who magnifies himself creates a cult culture in which a dear leader's ego is of paramount importance. This typically creates a fear-driven organization of sycophants. In contrast, a leader who magnifies her people, exposes their contributions, and appreciates their intelligence creates a culture in which she is not the center of attention and people trust that they are appreciated. This leader increases the individual happiness of each employee and thus increases the company's gross happiness.

The pushback I get from younger entrepreneurs is that some cultlike companies are successful. When I ask what kind of success they have achieved, the answer is invariably financial. Though *financial success* is a relative term and since many more cult companies perish than thrive, I cannot help but feel this is a very limited definition of success. There are many financially successful people who lie forgotten in the graveyard. More sit alone in their hillside mansions bereft of tenderness from others or compassion from anyone. Success involves the whole person and his or her set of accomplishments. At the risk of sounding like Jacob Marley, one's impact on the bottom line is less important than one's impact on humans, yet both are related; they are not mutually exclusive. Tiger Woods accomplished much on the golf course and nearly destroyed it in the bedroom. Mike Tyson was an accomplished boxer but will be remembered only for his facial tattoo and cannibalistic tendencies in the ring. O.J. Simpson squandered everything he ever earned and now, languishing in prison, is the source for jokes, not admiration.

Mother Teresa, in contrast, was not a financial success but was successful at everything else.

People do need money, and so an entrepreneur has to understand the right and wrong ways of providing financial incentives to help guide the corporate body. Restricted stock units, also known as golden handcuffs, are perhaps the worst incentive plan yet devised. Foremost, these stock grants are bribes that are based on the idea that if you stay with the company a certain number of years, you will be a virtuous and involved employee. Time has shown that this more likely creates bored, angry, and resentful employees who linger and create a drag on the company to get free money. It is a nearly perfect ingratitude machine. The reward is unassociated with what matters: the success of the company and the cohesiveness of the employees, the ability to improve, grow, and sustain one another. The reward comes by virtue of endurance, not contribution.

Stock options, by contrast, are a very appropriate form of compensation. An employee's finances are improved by what he contributes to the company. Barring uncontrollable external factors such as the Great Recession, each employee's personal involvement in the company directly affects her future gain. This incentive system causes people to want to work together better, not simply to be the last old person standing next to the water cooler. Closer and deeper employee collaboration drives workers to reinforce the corporate culture and focus intently on the mission and vision.

Corporate happiness, being about people, attracts the right employees. The microchip industry is highly competitive, and great employees, highly creative people, are instrumental to winning market share. You hire the best people, not greedy ones who want to work there to bump up their personal wealth. Such candidates lack the motivation and cultural awareness necessary to contribute effectively. Like a VC-infused entrepreneur, they focus on wealth, not on the mission. Some candidates are surprised when I tell them that I am not there to make them rich but to help them become better people. Some candidates get it, and the rest find work elsewhere.

Does this work? Micrel has a voluntary employee turnover rate that is about half of the industry average, and last year over 60 of our hires were rehires: people who left Micrel and then decided that life was better here.

This is where helping people, servant leadership, altruism, and compassion drive great companies: great employees are driven by their happiness, not by unmetered greed. Similarly, great entrepreneurs are driven by great accomplishments and great employees.

As you can see, synergies abound when it comes to focusing on people, and this makes the shortsighted desire in Silicon Valley to offshore everything mystifying. There is no argument that in the short term at least one can have products made more cheaply and technical support provided more economically in other parts of the world. Yet never do the spreadsheets show the long-term lost opportunity costs that come from losing employees' trust and not creating a more completely integrated company.

If an entrepreneur spends a lot of his time creating a business composed of people who are deeply stitched together, who feel respected and appreciated, he loses much of that internal goodwill—that gross corporate happiness—when he outsources. Nobody feels trust when she believes her job might be the next one exported to India or China.

Employee trust often boils down to the entrepreneur's objective and whether it is a short-term financial gain or a long-term enterprise-building mission. If your objective is like that of Cisco and other electronic equipment companies—to not manufacture anything—outsourcing may be appropriate and saying so up front eliminates employee mistrust. But if your objective is to have a happy company that employs people fully engaged in the entrepreneur's mission, it is not the way to go. Outsourcing leads to more difficult operations, and this creates friction and inefficiencies. It detracts from fast, efficient internal communications. It adds unnecessary delays in product rollouts. It cheats employees of their potential work happiness, which in the long run cheats stockholders out of a return on their investment.

Micrel is a U.S.-based company and thus an oddity in our industry for having fabrication facilities not only in the United States but in the business-unfriendly state of California. We pay taxes that could legally be avoided. We could withdraw from the Silicon Valley area. We could do a lot of things conventionally. But by staying we improve operations between our divisions. We create a more relaxed work environment while improving productivity by keeping staff in close proximity. We add to the region's commonweal. Just as I try to directly help any Micrel employee who needs my assistance in doing his or her job, so too does Micrel help Silicon Valley.

Just as paying forward a kindness launches a great deal of delight in a Starbucks drive-through lane, onshoring launches greater community happiness. For every person you employ, you affect seven other people locally. The chip designer buys a new car. The fab operations manager eats at the local restaurant. The tech support engineer buys her new laptop at Fry's Electronics down the street. Your decision about who you employ includes where they live and how the wealth you create together is spent and invested. Outsourcing as little as possible means contributing geometrically to San Jose, where Micrel is based, to Silicon Valley, to America.

Imagine if the other "American" microchip companies could say the same thing.

More important than sustaining the local, state, and national economy is the sustaining of quality. Whatever you outsource is no longer completely within your control. Certainly, contractual agreements and a collection of several different suppliers mitigate such risk. But keeping your operations in-house and onshore ensures that you have complete control over the quality of the product from design, to manufacturing, to distribution, to support. In part this explains why so many product designers turn to Micrel as their primary vendor: their products' reputation is only as good as the components inside, and Micrel never compromises on quality because we don't have to.

Aside from all these long-term benefits, there is the exponential development of talent. Employees, being the body of the organization, have to be able to do the job. Outsourcing noncore competencies has practical value, but anything associated with the core of the business—the mechanics of creating, selling, and supporting a product—is best insourced. It may be more expensive in the short term, but the integration of talent and knowledge creates a sum greater than its parts. It improves the entire muscle memory of the corporate body. In turn, this amplifies the company's core competence while eliminating vulnerability from outside organizations.

Onshoring communicates a lot to your employees. It is an action that says that management is committed to them, to the company they work for, to the community they live in, and to the country they love. It is an action that speaks louder than words and an operational communication to all employees.

When all is said and done about the human condition, communication is all we have and is what leads to a unified organization. An entrepreneur with a dream acquires no funding, no followers, no employees, and no revenues unless she can communicate that dream. It is the organizational mind channeling what the business's eyes perceive to achieve the heart's objectives. Entrepreneurs learn quickly that the one thing they must do in the beginning is also the one thing they will do more of over time, and that is communicate.

Communicating begins by shutting up.

Listening is an acquired skill some people never attain. It is human nature to want to be understood, and entrepreneurs—passionate about their vision of things to come—are excited to tell everyone about it. We have all met them here in Silicon Valley: the founder who acts more like a nonstop advertisement for his product, never inhaling long enough for his audience of one to interject. Without listening, he relates the wrong information at the wrong level of detail to an increasingly irritated person. It communicates that he is not at all interested in understanding the other person's needs, and he conveys that as plainly as he would if he were shouting the words aloud.

We have two ears and one mouth for a reason and should use them proportionately. Entrepreneurs often try to be an educator or professor rather than being a student, absorbing input from employees throughout the company. Unfortunately, most executives who think they know it all immediately enter instruction mode. People want you to hear what they have on their minds. They don't want you to teach them or be their god.

Because of this, entrepreneurs should seek to understand before seeking to be understood. This applies to sales pitches, R&D meetings, investor conferences—every aspect of running the entrepreneur's business and life. It communicates to people—the arms, legs, and hands of his enterprise—that the entrepreneur has authentic interest in them, their jobs, their roadblocks, their aspirations. It makes them a fully integrated part of the entrepreneur's mission.

But there is listening and then there is *listening*. Some people passively listen in order to formulate a rebuttal. Others actively listen. Steven Jobs was legendary for listening so intently—looking like Spock in a turtleneck sweater—that it scared some people. He was an active listener. He absorbed every word; quickly summarized the intent, meaning, and content; and spoke directly to the issue. He was willingly involved in what the other person had to say.

A willing listener is someone who truly wants to understand what is being said as opposed to merely absorbing dialogue. Willing listeners smile, reflect the other person's information, and are openly supportive. They project empathy, teach as part of their listening, and act kindly in response. Yes, it is listening to obtain information, but it is also listening to more deeply engage others and by doing that to encourage them to be open and reflective themselves.

A lack of active listening communicates a disregard for the employee. Imagine visiting your doctor and after he asks "How are you doing?" he stares a little past your head, not nodding, asking questions, or writing notes in your file. His lack of engagement communicates a general lack of interest in your health. But a doctor who sits on your hospital bed, pats your hand, repeats your symptoms back to you when you list them, and asks questions about your family medical history communicates authentic interest, and this creates trust. The patient is comforted, and the doctor learns more than does his less engaged peer.

Doctors have also noticed that patients don't always provide all the pertinent information and that active listening tends to surface more critical data. A passively listening doctor might miss a key symptom that a patient is shy about discussing or did not think was important. Not only does active listening make the other person more relaxed and participative, it also gives the listener more insight, and with that insight he makes better decisions. An entrepreneur is involved with each department and every division and listens to every employee she can. By doing this she creates in her mind a complex matrix of the state of the business, the product, and the market and as a result makes wiser decisions and increases the probability of achieving her vision. All it takes is a little time. The payoff leads to greater coordination of the corporation through improved feedback from all body parts. It increases entrepreneurial control.

Praise. Servant leadership. Respect. Fairness. Frugality with resources. Listening. These are the means by which the mind orchestrates the movement of the corporate body.

LESSONS

- It doesn't matter how able an entrepreneur is if the organization doesn't listen.
- Communication is a major part of an entrepreneur's job: communicating the mission, the values, the policies, and the market realities of the company.
- Agreement between the entrepreneurial mind and heart is absolutely essential. Otherwise the corporate body will not respond to either one.
- Head count is less important than the way employees work together.

- Entrepreneurs preserve and grow employee happiness, acknowledging that money is a factor but not *the* factor.
- Coordination requires the corporate body to receive and willingly act on coordinating instructions.
- Communicating begins by shutting up. We have two ears and one mouth for a reason; use them proportionately.
- A good place to start learning how to lead and communicate is outside a corporation, particularly in nonprofit organizations in which money is not a motivator.
- When the CEO shares pain and risk, employees trust him or her and trust must always come from the very top.
- Corporate regimentation exists to create the disciplines necessary to ensure uniformity of action.
- Corporate frugality starts with the entrepreneur, and it is mechanically impossible to be too frugal.
- Restricted stock units (aka golden handcuffs) are perhaps the worst incentive plan yet devised.
- Onshoring creates greater community happiness, which pays long-term corporate and talent dividends.

PART II

ENTREPRENEURIALISM: BUILDING COMPANIES THAT LAST THROUGH THE AGES

CHAPTER 5

Nurturing Corporate Culture

A frustrated member of the executive team shoved a fistful of one-dollar bills at me during a staff meeting.

He was both an executive and a friend, someone I had recruited from within the industry for his talent and his drive. The only problem was that he, like many men in the booming microchip industry of that era, had a mouth from which expletives erupted with consistent frequency. He was a great fit in Micrel's culture except for this one habit, which is against the company's policies.

This put me in a tough position. I wanted him on the team. I knew he would make significant contributions to the company's success. But since foul language is against Micrel's culture of upholding everybody's dignity, he needed to curb his swearing. Statistically speaking, this did not seem possible, for I could not recall a single conversation with him that didn't contain colorful words. Hiring and then firing him would not do, and he was immune to threats. But he wasn't immune to a challenge. I told him that from now on he would pay me one dollar every time I caught him swearing and that the funds would go to staff party expenses.

He took the bait.

After a week or so, he started holding on to his one-dollar bills when a cashier handed him change, and daily I headed home with a few extra dollars for the party fund. It got to the point where he asked for singles at the bank, knowing his workday involved giving them to me. He had not quit cussing, but it was becoming a nuisance to him and comedic relief to everyone who witnessed our daily transactions.

During one staff meeting, he absentmindedly let slip a vulgarity. He immediately caught himself and in reaction let loose another. He was so surprised that he had tripped twice in rapid succession that a third profanity spilled out. The meeting room fell silent as he stared at me and I waited. He shoved a hand into his pocket, extracted a sizable wad of rumpled one-dollar bills, and poked them at me. I took all of them—for current offenses and a few future penalties—and put them in my pocket.

The staff meeting went on without him letting loose again. By the time he retired from Micrel, his swearing had pretty much ceased.

Corporate culture is the one essential ingredient that entrepreneurs must get right early on. I know of companies that have survived the violent changes of their markets because their cultures guided every employee through times of great transition. I know of no company with a weak or ill-defined culture that lasted, period.

Corporate culture is composed of the principles by which a company is going to guide itself. Employees are largely autonomous, and no entrepreneur would want or have the time to hold the hand of every team member. Corporate culture becomes the guidelines within which everybody participates. This is the same mechanism that societies around the world use. A set of guiding principles, established by tradition or religion or law, are taught to everyone, and everyone aside from outcasts, eccentrics, and criminals abides by those principles. Without culture, societies and companies would collapse or devolve into anarchy.

Corporate anarchy isn't profitable.

Defining the corporate culture is one of the very first things an entrepreneur should formalize. A marketing strategist I know warns his executive clients that they must define and communicate their brands because in the absence of a brand definition, the market defines the brand and the market is not always kind. Similarly, an entrepreneur who fails to define her corporate culture in effect delegates the creation of the business's ethics to all of her employees, who, being individuals, will not agree on much and probably never formalize the cultural imperatives. You can control it yourself, or it will be done without control. A baker who lets random strangers select his ingredients will bake truly awful bread.

An entrepreneur needs to be up front, have a clear strategy about his corporate culture, and articulate the expected cultural norms. It can be as simple as the legendary HP Way or be spelled out as it is in Google's *Ten Things We Know to Be True*. But it has to be communicated, understood, and repeated at every opportunity.

Micrel's culture, like that of most entrepreneur-founded companies, is a reflection of the founder's personal ethics. Four absolutes guide Micrel's culture: honesty, integrity, the dignity of every individual, and doing whatever it takes. All other actions are based on these principles, and every employee needs no further instruction (though we do talk about culture frequently at Micrel). A culture based in honesty is reflected in the way employees treat one another, our suppliers, and our customers. Integrity assures that promises made—delivery schedules, quality guarantees, and pricing promises—are kept. Guarding everybody's dignity—showing respect for every individual regardless of his or her position in the company—means that all the very different people want to stay at Micrel and continue reinforcing the culture.

Because people are so different, a common corporate culture is fundamental to sane operations. We are all raised with somewhat different values. I was taught that swearing is rude, whereas my one-dollar senior executive had other thoughts about cursing. For him to work with me, my other executives, and all his subordinates, he had to adapt to our culture, and it was my job to find a way to instigate the change.

Culture is like sheet music for a choir. All the chorale members have a different range, a personal internal tempo, and individual tonal variations. Without a pitch whistle and sheet music, even the Mormon Tabernacle Choir would sound horrible, with everyone singing his or her own song in his or her own key. Culture is the process of harmonizing a choir of very individual employees so that their product, their output, resonates into something more beautiful than they could produce on their own.

This all begins with entrepreneurs, many of whom struggle to assemble global treaties on work life. The United Nations couldn't produce some of the all-inclusive documents that entrepreneurs have developed to stage their corporate cultures. It has been said that nobody really knows the key to success, but the key to failure is trying to please everybody. Attempting to create an all-encompassing culture document that pleases everybody is a failed project even before it starts.

Entrepreneurs should know that their corporate culture is, and probably should be, a reflection of themselves—of their values and their beliefs about business. Unless a man is a complete reprobate, odds are that his set of values, crafted for his persona and his industry, will be the best guide for the company. Foremost, his vision can be created only by using his understanding of the mission.

Any culture that he does not embrace will eventually dissolve his passion, and soon enough it won't be his company anymore. More important, if the "defined" corporate culture does not agree with his, his actions won't agree with the defined culture. Employees who understand the corporate culture yet see the CEO acting contrary to that culture will lose faith and not abide by it either. The Catholic Church has lost many members because the actions of a few priests were not corrected by the Vatican, and that was a from-the-top violation of the church's documented culture.

Integrity is the cornerstone of an entrepreneur's cultural discipline. He has to develop a transparency that allows employees to believe that he adheres to the culture and its rules. If employees who travel are banished to coach and he flies first class, the employees will dismiss his other directions. If he promises raises and doesn't deliver, his word becomes worthless. The biggest danger an entrepreneur faces is when he is inconsistent with his decisions and in his directions. Perhaps it is a sign of modern times, but I often surprise people with Micrel's integrity when we deliver. Our consistency is surprising in an industry that moves so fast that people are tempted to take shortcuts. Consistency has caused our company to be successful and allowed us to always do what we said we were going to do.

Lacking a defined and viable corporate culture is not a barrier to financial success, but it *is* a barrier to entrepreneurial success. Some people get lucky. Some would-be entrepreneurs happen to envision the exact right product at the exact right moment in market history and swiftly capitalize on it. But every lucky streak ends: not every card can be a winner, and even pool sharks can't sink a three-bank combo every time. Those lucky few tend not to last, and their success is merely monetary. Entrepreneurs live to accomplish their missions, and short-term financial gain is secondary. Building a lasting corporation and a culture that perpetuates it is an accomplishment.

One of the reasons to correctly define a corporate culture early on is that it tends to become self-perpetuating. Once a set of values and attitudes are shared among a group of people, they tend to reinforce it and associate with others who share those values. A company with a certain culture will celebrate that culture and hire people who appear to be a good fit, which is shorthand for being culturally aligned. Similarly, people not aligned with the culture will leave for other opportunities, and a strong leader has to be prepared to fire those who don't exit soon enough (you know who needs to go, so don't waste time making it happen). With the feedback loop occurring, changes to corporate culture become more difficult, for better or worse. Old-timers at Hewlett-Packard, people who knew Bill and Dave personally, still hold dear the culture they adopted despite a series of outside CEOs who all but decimated the HP Way. Conversely, an entrepreneur who sees that the culture in his company is not compatible with his vision will find it difficult to change the course of that culture. Top-down pressure will go only so far.

Communicating the culture is a challenge every entrepreneur will face. Written words are rarely sufficient. People, being visual creatures, understand concepts better if they can visualize them. It is one thing to say that Micrel is based on honesty; it is another to discuss acts of honesty at an annual all-hands meeting. Most companies use their internal communications to echo stories about how various parts of the corporate mission have been exemplified. When a company is starting, all these communications—these instances of positive group feedback—come from the entrepreneur. But even in mature enterprises, the CEO remains involved in this loop, often approving which stories are broadcast throughout the business.

Praising adherence is an example of leading cultural thought. However, employees can move ahead of the entrepreneur.

Early on, many Micrel employees wanted the company to go public. Their stock options would become more liquid, and they could see a brighter future for themselves. But it took a while to get there, and I did not communicate that. Employee expectations were moving ahead of Micrel's situation, and the employees assumed I was on the verge of taking the company public despite my never having said I would. At about the five-year mark, our employees began to doubt that we were ever going to become a publicly traded company. Many became disenchanted.

To keep morale high, I had to tell them that it was our intention to go public and articulate that in a way that had some measureable time period that the employees would accept. The problem was that I wasn't able to get the company ready for an IPO as quickly as the employees would have liked. I wanted the company to be at a certain revenue level, at a certain earnings horizon, before we launched an IPO to assure that Micrel was sustainable. The delays resulted in people accusing me of never wanting to take the company public. I had in a sense unintentionally violated my own cultural claims. Some employees saw me as dishonest and lacking integrity.

Transparency becomes one of the essential disciplines for an entrepreneur. It isn't because he lacks fidelity, and the employees are not unduly suspicious. It is because where there is a gap in knowledge, people write their own stories. This bit of human nature can cause havoc if leaders—whether entrepreneurs, enterprise CEOs, or presidents of countries—fail to be informative and transparent. If the information gap intersects with the defined culture, the culture takes a hit as well and it is difficult to rebuild it. Yet things change, companies change, and markets change. Entrepreneurs must occasionally edit their vision, and this requires keeping employees informed lest they write their own stories to complete the picture. As long as they see that you are adjusting your plan, they'll stick with you and continue to embrace your culture.

This sounds like a lot of work, but it isn't. Defining a corporate culture does take a bit of soul-searching and a little careful composition. The rest falls into the categories of communicating—which is the bulk of an entrepreneurial CEO's job—and understanding how change should be communicated to the team. If goals are properly set and the culture is reasonably well crafted, most daily work and even significant organizational transitions will go off without a hitch.

The real work is managing change, which does involve managing culture, which in turn involves constant communications and small changes to prevent large-scale culture shock. In Silicon Valley, there is a level of erratic executive behavior that is plainly reckless. Market shifts cause CEOs and start-up entrepreneurs to slam on the brakes and jerk the steering wheels of their companies. Their employees, investors, and other passengers are battered as the company skids out of control and crashes. Part of the problem is the disruption of the corporate culture, the failure of the CEO to recognize change early and calmly signal that she will steer the company in another direction.

I won't oversimplify the process because change is always traumatic. Any time you make a change, it is going to be disturbingly disruptive to the company. However, change is inevitable, and in the high-tech industry, change is constant. Most of the time it involves foreseeable shifts in demand as new technologies drive new markets the way smartphones and tablets have replaced laptops as the preferred consumer computing platforms. Other shifts are gut-wrenching, requiring a company to fundamentally change its mission and with that its vision of how to achieve the mission as well as associated cultural traits.

When employees have a cultural foundation designed to accomplish what is best for the company, you will avoid the chaotic consequences of change, both sudden and gradual. Micrel has successfully transitioned at least five times in the last 30 years. We started in an era when a computer still occupied an entire room and the big ones were water-cooled. Today, you carry more computing horsepower in your pocket than mainframes once had. If we had not watched the market, gauged the changes, and picked our specialties, we would not have survived such tectonic shifts in the semiconductor industry. If we had not anticipated the changes, we would not have planned appropriately and I would have had to slam on the brakes while jerking Micrel's steering wheel to avoid crashing. If we had not been proactive, the cultural shifts would have been too sudden and the employees would have lost faith. Instead, we signaled our turns and used our enduring cultural principles to drift through the corners of our markets.

Maintaining cultural alignment begins with listening and starts at the top. Micrel made certain product decisions that were significant changes for us, ones that rippled through engineering and sales, where years of designing and vending one type of technology would eventually be replaced with radically new technologies and markets. We started with our own board of directors, letting each member speak to the issue and, by participating, come to an agreement on what was best for Micrel. Once the new strategic direction was decided on, everybody in the company needed to be educated about the long-range planning and why change was necessary. Because employees saw the thought put into strategic decisions and noted the consensus within the board, their worry about the change was reduced and our course corrections appeared to be a calm transition, not a panic-induced reaction.

This is where an entrepreneur's workload actually increases: thinking about change execution and all the unintended consequences of change. When we added digital communications products to Micrel, it could have been viewed by some as abandoning our former core of analog products, but that was not the case, and all the stakeholders—employees, investors, and customers—needed to understand this. Failing to communicate the change would have left some with the false impression that Micrel was forsaking them. Entrepreneurial CEOs must think clearly about all unintended consequences, all ramifications associated with planned change, and take into account what cultural issues are woven into the fabric of the company.

The board and I made a big decision when we chose to move into the communications sector, which is definitely bigger and better than analog semiconductors. But doing that required a whole new set of talent and very different technology. To still the churning waters and keep the Micrel corporate culture humming, I brought everybody together. We talked about the market and endlessly discussed the upsides and downsides. I gave every employee the pros and cons of wading into digital communications, which in 1997 was at the front edge of Internet consumerization and was a constantly shifting sea of standards and market leaders.

There were some very big concerns. It was a huge change because communications was a completely different business from the one at which Micrel had excelled. The shift caused many employees whose entire careers and very livelihood was based in analogs to fret. Others saw the growing dot-com era and recognized that not being part of that market would be a wasted opportunity. It was my job to manage employees' expectations and do that within Micrel's cultural framework. Our dedication to respect for all individuals meant respecting their talent, their jobs, their futures, and their fears. Because we engaged in dialogue by making it a two-way conversation about markets, opportunities, and Micrel's future, their thoughts were fully recognized, and in the long run we had passionate employee participation. An autocratic CEO who would have announced marching orders without discussion would have caused Micrel to collapse.

Entering the digital communications semiconductor market was a good decision and a great ride, but Micrel got caught in the dot-com bust like everyone else. Five short years lapsed between making the decision to enter the communications space and having to deal with massive change in the tech fallout. When the dot-com bubble burst, we lost half our revenue almost instantaneously, and we had to shift gears once again. Our employees, who had just survived one roller coaster ride, were flung onto another. It put a lot of pressure on the company to speed shift like that.

We had to shut down one facility, though this had been a delayed decision and did not surprise many Micrel employees. We remained profitable despite the market meltdown. Our only unprofitable year followed when the facilities closure write-downs landed on the books. There were other consolidations, and it was up to me to properly articulate to our team that we were still succeeding and that it was due to them and the Micrel culture. Other companies were in bankruptcy, but we were only a little unprofitable and had no reason to be so the next year. We had already weathered the worst of the dot-com bust and had our sights on regaining momentum. Micrel had the confidence it needed because of the solid string of successes it had and the culture that had facilitated those wins. We were stable because we had a stable culture.

A long-term cultural discipline that technology companies should acquire is dealing with change (some Silicon Valley swashbucklers believe in *embracing* change, but this often leads them to fad-following self-destruction). If change will be part of your corporate strategy or vision, you need to culturally condition your employees to accept it and constantly adapt. If it is not part of your strategy, it will occur anyway—albeit less frequently—and you will have to manage the collateral cultural shift in very sensitive ways.

Occasionally a CEO must change the culture. Sometimes the markets change so radically that what once led to growth in one market is not appropriate for growth elsewhere. The longer a culture has been established, the longer it will take to change. This creates a conflict when cultural change is induced by a board of directors who want to replace the CEO. Investors and the board often are looking for rapid changes in the fortunes of the company. If a well-established culture exists and must change to meet the new corporate direction, nothing will change rapidly. Hewlett-Packard has—or perhaps I should say *had*—a profound culture that served it well as a technology design company. Their culture led them into many businesses, mostly profitable, and HP was universally lauded as a purveyor of indestructible hardware. Deep inside HP this has not changed.

Yet Hewlett-Packard abandoned its history of promoting CEOs from within, and a series of outsiders changed the company, though not the core culture. They wanted HP to run in new directions and change its mode of being profitable—from designing great products to being the least expensive vendor. The company was never known for its software, but one of the later CEOs made his stand by declaring that HP would be a software company. He then embarked on an acquisition spree that in the long run included a multi-billion-dollar write-down. He did not examine the unintended consequences that involved cultural change and lasted only a year in his job.

Changing a culture requires small steps, not giant leaps. It requires demurely deemphasizing obsolete aspects of the culture while slowly introducing new ones. It is a process, not an event. Picture all the immigrants fleeing war-torn third world countries who landed in New York City and the cultural shock they endured.

Tearing out hunks of an existing culture always meets with resistance, as Native Americans demonstrated.

At Micrel we never had to drastically alter our culture because it is based on universal, humanistic principles. Yet we have had to adapt to industry changes that were revolutionary. By setting our culture on principles that are part of human interaction, we ensured civil collaborations that created and expanded trust vertically throughout Micrel and horizontally from suppliers to customers. Entrepreneurs need to define and nurture their corporate culture, but they should not attempt to micromanage every detail of every interaction.

Culture should not prevent a company from exploring and growing. Thus, overly complex, long-winded, and expansive policy statements tend to muddy cultural waters instead of clarifying them. Micrel's two top principles—honesty and integrity—never keep an employee from seeking new ways of making our customers successful. Treating people with respect and doing whatever it takes actually accelerate the process. This short set of corporate cultural elements has enabled Micrel employees to make informed and sage decisions without managerial hand-holding. None of those guideposts have inhibited Micrel's creativity or flexibility. It has been said that simple rules lead to complex and intelligent thinking and that complex rules lead to simple and stupid thinking. The same thing applies to the principles behind a corporate culture.

Such simple principles also last through the undulations of markets, shifts in technology, and even the replacement of CEOs if the incoming leader embraces the existing culture. Culture has a pacifying effect by which people can look to their culture—whether it is societal, religious, or corporate—and find their way through tough times. People are always upset when change occurs. When the CEO announces a new corporate mission, when you bring on a new boss, a new set of equipment, new software systems—any change is going to be frightening because it always comes with uncertainty. A sound corporate culture based on simple and humanistic principles will smooth transitions because employees have the guidance they need before they need it and have seen it in action. The culture reduces what might otherwise be viewed as chaos.

Where a strong culture really shines is in the confidence it inspires. A confident entrepreneur can take employees pretty far on his drive and charisma alone. But when an organization grows large enough that the founders cannot personally interact with all the employees on a daily basis, something else must stand in its place yet instill the same belief in success. A strong culture then becomes a perpetual motion machine, because the culture extends the entre-preneur's guidance, which breeds more confidence, which in turn reinforces the culture. The sense of competence and confidence the entrepreneur brought to the company sets the stage for the culture to grow, a process that then sustains itself.

It requires both confidence and competence. If an entrepreneur is confident but incompetent, employees will witness her mistakes and view her confidence as delusional or egotistical behavior, leading to corporate mutinies. People with competence but no confidence simply never become entrepreneurs, lacking the belief in their own success. They will never create the opportunity to build a corporate culture. Yet confidence, competence, and a culture defined to repeat success will convert the entrepreneur's abilities into lasting results.

There comes a moment in the growth of a company that makes the entrepreneur smile. When his confidence helps competent employees create products and generate growth, parts of his company begin running themselves. This is the first sign that the corporate culture has succeeded. The business continues running, continues growing, without the entrepreneur having to keep his hands on the steering wheel at every moment. Micrel was nearing its third birthday when I first recognized this. Despite its being profitable in the very first year, we had our growing pains and I was working as closely as I could with everyone in the organization. When our second profitable year came, our employees shifted from celebrating our good fortune to assuming this was how things were going to go from then on (and it did aside from one year during the dot-com implosion). In our third year, employees needed less and less of my input yet excelled. I started taking my hands off the steering wheel, and we didn't crash.

We were successful. The company was hitting on all cylinders. It was profitable; it was growing. Employees were happy, morale was good, turnover was low, and we executed well. The culture was vibrant because it was well defined and simple.

LESSONS

+ No company with a weak or ill-defined culture will last. Corporate anarchy isn't profitable.
+ A strong culture inspires organizational confidence and competence.
+ Corporate culture is composed of the principles by which a company is going to guide itself.
+ All-encompassing culture documents that attempt to please everybody are failed projects.
+ Integrity is the cornerstone of an entrepreneur's cultural discipline. Develop transparency and allow the employees to believe the rules.
+ Honesty comes from the mind. Integrity comes from the heart. This is doing what's right when nobody is watching.
+ Communicating culture is a challenge. Written words are rarely sufficient.

- Changing a culture requires small steps, not giant leaps.
- Managing change involves managing culture, which in turn involves constant communications.
- A cultural foundation designed to accomplish what is best for the company will prevent the chaotic consequences of change.

CHAPTER 6

Making People Important

"I feel more fulfilled, more successful now that I have changed my demeanor," is how I remember my formerly foul-mouthed senior executive summing up his growth at Micrel. "When I was at my previous company, I thought we had all sorts of freedom and I felt really open, great. Then I came here, and at first I felt restricted. I felt confined, thinking, 'This is too much like going to church every Sunday.'"

He did have a hard time adapting to our no-swearing policy and to the fact that Micrel's culture was significantly different from that of his previous employer and the semiconductor industry in general. He was also concerned because he initially viewed Micrel as not being a friendly place, and he continued to misperceive it that way until he decided to change. After a while and a small exchange of wealth via one-dollar bills, he got into the groove of our culture, muted his colorful vocabulary, and actually enjoyed working here more than anywhere else. People liked dealing with him more and more. He became a truly great employee and has found greater happiness even in his personal life.

Micrel has that effect on people because we pay attention to the fundamentals of human happiness. That lifts employees in ways no stock option or annual bonus check can. Micrel helps people become better people, and they return the favor by being better employees.

Paying attention to the things that are the basis of human happiness is why Micrel has a low turnover rate and many boomerang employees: ones who leave us and then come back after tasting the culture in other companies. Our boomerang employees often say things like, "Wow, that was too big of a sticker shock," after seeing how other companies value and devalue their employees. Some, mainly those who come to us straight out of college, did not think they liked it at Micrel and took jobs elsewhere. About half of them have come back because they discovered that what they first thought of as restrictive was actually liberating and that much of Silicon Valley works only on a financial basis, not a human one. Other employers took care of their wallets, but Micrel also took care of their hearts. Happiness comes from within, and no boss or corporate culture can *make* somebody happy. Yet a boss and his company can facilitate happiness and nurture innovation, allowing employees to be part of something that satisfies their innate human needs.

Truly happy people have found value in their existence. Something—whether love, community, achievement, or involvement—has made their time on earth important, and thus they are important themselves. Most people discover their hearts are at peace when they are in service to others: their children, their aging parents, or even strangers at the local homeless shelter. Employees who dutifully come to the office, work their exact eight hours, mindlessly follow detailed procedures, and try only hard enough to meet their management by objectives (MBO) scores do not perceive themselves as valuable. Employees who happily rush to an office where they have the permission to innovate, feel connected to others in the organization, and exceed any MBO expectations *know* they have value.

One of the pillars of Micrel's culture is respect for everybody and his or her dignity. This includes the no-swearing policy that eventually transformed my profane executive. People cannot feel important if they work in a hostile environment or even one that makes them uncomfortable, as swearing can make some people feel. Nor is their self-perception of value increased by office politics, backbiting, or even simple rudeness. A bucket without any holes can carry a lot of water, but if you keep punching holes in that bucket, it won't hold any and you'll find yourself perpetually filling it because it is always leaking. As humans, we choose to either help fill buckets or perforate them. We either elevate our fellow humans and our coworkers or we drag them down.

Two of entrepreneurs' top jobs are to fill the buckets and to keep other people from splitting them, to nurture a supportive culture and to keep destructive people out of it.

An amazing thing occurs in an organization in which mutually assured happiness is common: everyone appears to be filling the other person's bucket, not just his or her own. Employees constantly ask, "How can I help you?" instead of avoiding the extra work that assisting others entails. Nobody is poking holes in others but instead is carrying water for his or her team. They are proactive not only in their work but in how they provide value to everyone else. Since truly happy people have found value in their existence and in helping others, an organization of bucket fillers tends to be bursting with happy folks.

It is a bit easier to tell when unhappiness is the rule. Unhappy people have lost sight of their value. Without value, they feel disconnected from others and their self-perception is diminished. You can also be unhappy by virtue of a bad incident—say, a family member being ill and suffering—mainly because you feel helpless and are facing a situation in which you are not adding value. When we have more obstacles to overcome than we can, hopelessness can clobber us. Yet it is the same issue. When you help others and see the results, your happiness increases. When you cannot help others, you sense a lack of value. When your world seems to be in turmoil, you cannot even see when your contributions help others and the same lack of value appears all-encompassing.

Adversity is like manure in that it stinks but helps us grow. In a helpful, nurturing culture, adversity's duration is shorter and the people who help are lifted by seeing their contributions work. Many people go to church not only because of their religious beliefs but also for the self-reinforcing fellowship that derives from being associated with people who you know are willing to help you and whom you are willing to help. Aside from theology, why should a corporation be less helpful, less nurturing, and less effective than a church or even a large family?

Mutually ensured success is part of this arrangement. We all want to succeed. We want the best for ourselves and our families, whether those families are by blood or by marriage or are simply the people we choose to be with. Family, church, the company one works for—no person is an island. We need to be treated with respect, dignity, and a sense of our importance regardless of where we are or which group of people we are with at the moment. It is the familial elements that make someone feel important in any group of people. We all like to hear our names spoken. We like to be referred to in a positive way, not in a degrading way. We all like feeling that we contribute and have value. Even the most destitute homeless people sleeping on dirty city streets want to believe they have value.

A recurring problem that is amplified in some organizations is that value is too often measured in a one-sided manner. Some corporate cultures drive an attitude of WIIIFM: what is in it for me.

People in such organizations love value provided that they are the recipients. They look upon humans as valueless unless those people provide value to them. But like a selfish lover, the other person giving soon gives up and provides his or her affection to someone who reciprocates. In companies without a culture of mutually assured success, people soon quit trying to help at all. In companies like Micrel, people thrive by helping.

One's attitude toward people in general determines whether one fills buckets or punches holes in them. I could view a person who works for a competitor as an enemy or as a head of a family just trying to provide for her children. Which way is better if your goal is to build a nurturing culture in which people actively help one another? "I won't talk to you because you work for my competitor and thus are my enemy" is very different from saying, "You are providing for your family. You are adding value. You are contributing to the economy. You are contributing to society. How would you like to work for a company that recognizes that?"

Sadly, much of Silicon Valley equates money with happiness. Money can buy a little transient joy or even add to your self-perceived value when you give it away, but money is not happiness itself. Money doesn't create value, yet the Silicon Valley mantra centers on getting rich. "I'll be happy if I am a millionaire by age 30" is not an unheard phrase. Silicon Valley, for all the cool things we invent and do, holds an obsessively materialistic view of success. Yet as with happiness, success comes from within.

Some companies do churn out happiness and success. Google is the current poster child for a different form of corporate thinking. People come to Google not just for a good salary but because they see large-scale change occurring on a daily basis. They see how Google's inventiveness has simplified lives, educated people, expanded human understanding, and even made us laugh. People who work at Google—and at Micrel—are driven less by money and more by doing interesting and important things. By changing a market or changing the world, individual employees witness their value and strive for more of the same. When their teammates stumble, they want to help because they know their fellow employee is just as likely to advance with a little assistance.

Two barriers to employee happiness, oddly, are money and time, and Silicon Valley holds the wrong priorities about both. They want lots of money, and they want it quickly. Silicon Valley success has in no small way become an engine of unhappiness because very few people there will get rich and fewer will do so quickly. Impatience and the impermanence it entails create Buddhist-style frustrations based on unfulfilled desires and hence a desire to quit early. Fixation on money obscures doing well at one's mission, and in the long run this produces an empty soul. Materialistic goals are not bad, but they become bad when they make achieving happiness impossible. It all begins and depends on your view—inward or outward. Focusing on yourself makes getting rich quick seem desirable, though the payoff rarely comes and is disappointing when it does. Focusing on others has instant and long-lasting rewards: "What can I do with my resources, with the skills that I have? Can I help? Can I become a value to anyone else?"

In this area, Silicon Valley luck has polluted some people's perspective. The Internet—that vast, always changing abstraction—has created a lot of opportunity and has also created instant billionaires. It makes everybody believe that you can get rich quick, just as every shower singer thinks he can be the next American Idol. But their financial success comes mainly from luck—the timing of their perception of the market—not necessarily from accomplishing a noble mission. Their wealth comes too quickly and before they're ready. It has tempted many into lavishness that fizzles when their momentary success is supplanted by the next big thing. They never learn to build an organization that consistently achieves, flourishes in bad times, and gives back to all the employees on a daily basis. They start running before they have learned to walk. They hit the lottery but still haven't tied their shoes.

Outside of Silicon Valley, financial success requires building solid cultures that increase employee happiness, and that takes time. Nobody was born a blacksmith; blacksmiths have to be apprentices first. Mother Teresa wasn't born a saint but earned the right to be called one through selfless devotion to suffering people. Some Silicon Valley companies are like the young professional athletes we have seen hauled off to jail. They received the wrong rewards before earning the sensibility to use their wealth wisely and then squandered their temporary fame. Honors too often don't come to the right people in their lifetimes: Mother Teresa, Mahatma Gandhi, Winston Churchill, Lincoln. Though they did great things, the worth of their acts was not recognized immediately. That happened when people looked back at what they did and understood the scope of the achievements. They were eventually recognized for the greatness of their deeds, not how much cash they stowed in a vault.

Yet these people were followed. Volunteers followed Mother Teresa into the slums of Calcutta. The British people lined up to follow Churchill's wartime resolve. A nation followed Lincoln through the trauma of civil war and finally to the redemption of emancipation. Who has devotedly followed the latest pop singer or paper billionaire aside from people wanting money, the same people who vanish the moment fame and money fade? Leaders create a sense of purpose, a sense of community, and a sense of mission toward which people happily strive.

A leader makes people feel important because the mission he is on is of great consequence, and by following him people create value in themselves—the core of happiness. Entrepreneurs have missions, but if they express those missions in terms of stuffed pockets, they attract only people who want their pockets stuffed. If instead they communicate the importance of the mission, they attract and keep employees who create in themselves a sense of importance and happily strive to achieve the entrepreneur's or the company's mission. Employees must believe in the mission, however. If they don't believe in the vision, they derive no sense of value and never achieve happiness in their work. They find other ways to fill the void.

Engagement is an essential part of employees believing in the mission. An aloof "leader" does not communicate her vision well. Instead she must be engaged with everyone she wants to follow her. As vile as the man was, even Adolf Hitler knew he had to engage with the German people on a personal and passionate basis. Connecting with employees is essential to getting them to understand your mission and your vision for completing it. I constantly engage in conversations with everybody at Micrel, not just the select few in a mythical inner circle. A simple "Hi, how you doing?" when walking down a hallway can lead to a conversation, a connection, and the chance to discuss how people are achieving the Micrel mission. It doesn't matter who they are, their job titles, or how far up or down the corporate ladder they may be. Opening a conversation lets them know their contribution, no matter how modest, has led to achievement by the company and thus their own personal value through achievement. It also demonstrates respect for the individual since they have the CEO's ear. If the opportunity presents itself, it gives the entrepreneur a chance to provide servant leadership and help employees overcome obstacles. Even if there is nothing to discuss about work, there are opportunities to learn about the people: their hobbies, their families, their passions outside the office; this again lets them feel important through sharing.

Making the workplace an extension of the employees' homes is about making the employees as comfortable there as they are in their own living rooms. This isn't to say we bring snacks, beer, and a big-screen TV into every cubicle. But it does mean providing a relaxed and nurturing environment, removing artificial partitions—whether physical or organizational—and letting all the employees commune with one another as if they were all in the same family. It also means providing the flexibility, empathy, and assistance a family member would to make life at work pleasant.

Micrel has an employee whose one-way commute takes three and a half hours. He has to get up pretty early in the morning, and seven hours a day on the road—especially through some of the San Francisco Bay Area's worst beep-and-creep traffic—can be daunting. Since he is on the road so early, we have him leave early to miss the afternoon rush. He takes Fridays to work from home since his job allows for off-site and flexible scheduling.

Companies and entrepreneurs need to be flexible that way, adapting—within reason—the specific needs of employees as they would the specific needs of their children, and every parent knows that all his children are very different from one another. Our commuting employee doesn't have to drive in horrible afternoon traffic; otherwise it would take him five hours to get home. One Micrel employee got custody of his children after a divorce, but his children lived in a different state because of quirks in the court's order. This tough situation was eased by letting him periodically commute back and forth and telecommute from the out-of-state home so that he could see his children without missing a paycheck.

Leadership is the business of people, and no rigid policy can accommodate every personal situation. An inflexible organization—one that fails to treat people with dignity and humanity—will only collect robotic workers who adapt to organizational rigidity.

Passionate entrepreneurs with grand missions will never succeed with such employees.

Even in an environment in which employees can sense their own value, no employee is hired fully formed. We are all humans, and thus we all have weaknesses. It can be as simple as a lack of experience in one skill set or as bad as struggling with alcoholism. Employee development—and, as we shall see in a bit, leadership development—is a continual process of lifting employees, identifying where they can improve themselves, create an ever greater sense of value, and thus become happier. It certainly is not a one-time event.

The first step is to avoid amplifying those weaknesses. People don't like their inequities exposed. An organization that protects the dignity of its employees shuns belittling people for what they cannot do or do well, for those things are fixable. Likewise, falsely glorifying the mundane is a transparent attempt to artificially boost morale. Every dollar spent on such fallacious incentives is wasted and would be better invested in authentic improvements in addressing another employee's needs.

There are much better ways to grow a sense of self and the confidence that comes with it. Like most top executives, I hold weekly operations meetings. The people who attend are themselves leaders in their disciplines. They are experts but also have their doubts and worries, as all humans do. Part of our ritual is for someone to give a motivational talk at the end of the meeting. The talks (which can be mine when appropriate) don't have to be about Micrel, our jobs, or even our industry. But they have to provide inspiration by showing how someone, somewhere persevered and succeeded. The talks can be about history, current events, business, and personal family stories. When we share our insights into what it takes to succeed, the sense of mission and achievement is constantly presented as *possible*.

Blessed with these stories of achieving the possible, my ops staff then does the impossible.

Being positive first is very important to people. We all have worked in negative environments in which blame is the first order of business at every encounter. People in such companies operate more out of fear than out of achievement. The attitude is one of disrespect by assuming the fault should lie with someone else. That environment is toxic to the very nature of humans. In dealing with people, respecting them as individuals, where they are in life, and who they are as humans sets a stage of trust, not mistrust. Always having a negative or a critical approach causes employees to shut off in self-defense. Assuming the positive by opening a discussion—no matter how dreadful the underlying issue may be—by saying something uplifting sets the stage for a collaborative discussion in which we don't seek blame but a solution. Ending on a positive note reassures the employee that our goal is to achieve something together. Even if I have to bring up a negative issue, ending on a positive note—positive, then negative, then positive again—lets them know that our chat was to improve things and continue working toward our common mission. Also, positive working environments and culture help reduce common frustrations. Anger is a first cousin to frustration, and anger breeds discontent, which inhibits productive passion and communication. When we eliminate frustration, beautiful things happen.

Creating a sense of humanistic support within a company begins with hiring. Although every person has value, not everybody has value that is important to the company, and that value may be buried under years of negative, destructive issues. The hiring process is an entrepreneur's best chance to mold the organization by bringing in people who will fit into his culture, bring passion as well as talent to the mission, and contribute to supporting all employees.

One of the great missed opportunities in growing a business and hiring great employees is the lack of interdisciplinary exposure. Getting people to work together is the entrepreneur's job. Getting people from different teams, departments, and even divisions of a company in one room goes far toward creating a collaborative environment. Getting people from different arenas to interview prospective employees is valuable along the same lines. A candidate who on paper is a perfect technical fit in one department may be a poor cultural fit in general. A manager desperate to fill a slot with someone experienced in his or her field may not recognize other deficiencies.

Micrel maintains a policy of requiring that at least six people interview all candidates, and at least half of the interviewers must come from outside the department that has the open requisition. If the candidate will report to me, she is interviewed by the entire board of directors as well as by me. This melting pot of perspectives measures how the candidate will fit cross-functionally—how he will creatively collaborate in support of the entire company, not just his team or his boss. Each interviewer then creates a detailed write-up covering critical attributes, including general cultural fit. We evaluate candidates' growth potential, their personality, how they're dressed, their communication skills, and a half dozen other elements. Interviewers rate the candidate on a 10-point scale, and we won't hire anybody who doesn't have an aggregate score of at least 7. For critical positions and senior management, the hurdle may be set higher—up to 9 out of 10 points.

Finding employees who fit is better than trying to force fit employees into a company. But people are individuals, and very few new hires are going to fall into place like a jigsaw puzzle piece. Letting employees fit in, as opposed to compelling them to fit in, is part of employee nurturing. Facilitating them in finding their own ways to commune, collaborate, and achieve is not only a humane approach but one that produces motivated employees who develop their own sense of value. Hammering round pegs into square holes either strips the peg of its form or distorts the hole. Shoving an employee into a cultural mold will either break the employee, making him less passionate about his new home, or disrupt and weaken the culture. People will find their own fit in an organization when you allow them to discover their own sources and their own ways of adapting. Making the corporate culture so inflexible that people cannot find a way in which they personally fit in is noxious to both the culture and the employee.

One part of this process of allowing employees to find their fit is to provide ways of finding commonality with other employees, and it helps if the activities are designed to improve employees in general. Micrel engages employees on many fronts, from a wellness program that established a competition using pedometers to measure physical activity to bringing financial advisors in to coach employees on managing their wealth. Because there is interaction between employees, people find other people who share their interests, whether it is losing a few pounds or better managing their retirement accounts. People who commune while walking, talking, spiking volleyballs, or shooting a round of golf increase their feeling of being part of a family. They find others with whom they enjoy playing or working and naturally discuss business issues. They do this all on a much more human level than occurs in sterile companies that lack authentic human connections.

A willingness to try is critical to every employee's sense of value and one of the key things every entrepreneur and executive should look for. Only when people stretch do they reach their goals. In the process of hiring, any indication that people are unwilling to do a little extra, to reach a little farther, is an indication that they may be subpar employees. I ask myself if a candidate would pick a piece of paper off the floor and put it in the trash can without being asked (some executives think that is beneath them, and because of that attitude they work elsewhere). Are they willing to do things outside the office? Are they willing to work whatever hours are necessary to meet a deadline? Would they willingly come to the office at a particular hour or stay overnight? Are they the types who volunteer? Those are the people who are easy to work with and do whatever they need to do to get the job done.

The single biggest red flag an entrepreneur should watch for is complaining. Someone who complains is someone who is finding fault with others and not finding solutions to problems. Everybody has issues with work, and most of us have at least one honest complaint to make about a boss, coworker, or employer. However, a candidate who openly complains about any of them shows her disposition. A candidate who complains about more than one of these connections is often the center of the storm and reflects her poor collaboration skills onto everyone else. Even if 100 percent of their complaints are legitimate, their preference to openly gripe instead of enduring and adjusting shows they will probably bring their poisonous attitude into the company.

People who don't complain either have a lot of passion or are milquetoasts. The former are candidates worth examining more closely and are easy to spot. They smile freely, talk about contributing, show enthusiasm for many things and not just their job, and enjoy talking about what they have accomplished not for bragging rights but because their sense of value—their achievements—is something they are excited about.

The people who show their value and their enthusiasm often show their ability to think outside the box. Those who do not will expose their conventional thinking and conventional wisdom, offering nothing surprising. Yet questioning people about how they came to certain decisions may unveil an inquisitive, exploring nature and the way they applied it to problems. As we know, people are either in the box and staring at its six walls or are inspecting the outside of the box to understand where artificial limits lie. Ask them how they arrived at a particular decision or how they did what they were most proud of or what one thing they have accomplished that makes them feel set apart from others. By asking about their obstacles, how they evaluated the situation, and how they arrived at their decision, you can separate in- from out-of-the-box thinkers.

This tactic pays off handsomely. Micrel has earned more patents per engineer than just about any other company in our industry despite not being the largest semiconductor company around. This comes directly from Micrel's inventive nature and ability to hire innovative people. We do have a lot of creative thinkers, know how to find them, and don't settle for anything less. This applies to every department from engineering to sales, to marketing, to manufacturing, to accounts payable. It is the hiring process that exposes the true innovators, even in finance.

I interviewed a candidate for the comptroller position at Micrel. A standard question for such people is how quickly they think they can close the books at the end of a fiscal quarter, and the standard range for our industry is 10 to 20 days. The candidate said he could do it in 10 days but his goal was 5, which is unheard of. Naturally, that piqued my curiosity, and I grilled him on how he could possibly achieve such a feat. He told me his plan of action, and from his description I could tell he had examined the outside of this accounting box. He understood where the delays were, why they existed, and how they could be collapsed. The fact that his maximum time to close the books was the minimum for everyone else was amazing, but the fact that he had a plan for cutting that time in half was both astounding and viable.

One of the worst things entrepreneurs can do is to effectively hire and then ignore their people. It is like bringing a puppy home and not feeding it. Unappreciated employees feel the abandonment and respond accordingly. Entrepreneurs who fail to follow through do so because they don't have an authentic belief in the value of humans. I often fly into cities at night and perk up when I see suburban street lights below. I ponder the magnificence of that—all those lights that represent homes where families are sitting around the dinner table telling their day's stories and sharing their lives. Just that one thought makes me feel happy, a joy born from having lived my life connected to humanity—the people in those houses, living, existing, and doing their best to survive. I find myself thinking not about the worst people—the corrupt politicians or inner-city gangsters—but the best. I don't find myself wondering who will feather my bed but how I can give something back to those people doing what is right and making a difference, whether small or large.

When an entrepreneur views all the decent people in the world as important because they're adding value, he will nurture his employees differently. Since everybody should be treated with as much importance as you can possibly render to her, your employees should be treated that way. If a street beggar deserves our attention, should not your janitor, your secretaries, your engineers, and your executives? The more frequently you empathize with every human being and understand that we all struggle to succeed, the more relevant every person becomes to you. When people become important to you, you in turn become important to them.

Some managers and some executives are just the opposite. They are like rhinoceroses, parading around in armored skin, impenetrable and never vulnerable. They advertise an attitude that shouts, "You can't get to me!" Sometimes it is because of ego. Occasionally an entrepreneur can reach a status in life that makes her believe she is perfect. Other times entrepreneurs know they are not, and to protect their sense of value, they build defenses and grow thick skins. They are constantly on guard and automatically suspect everyone. They remain untouchable.

And by being untouchable, they forget how to touch others except to hurt them.

Humans prefer people who care, and that includes their managers. They appreciate someone who listens, who wants to help and provide flexibility in the workplace to accommodate human needs outside the office. People prefer feeling valued to feeling as if they were a threat. They appreciate being trusted to think for themselves, not being told how to do everything. To be that kind of leader requires being connected to people, and you cannot connect with people who have thick skin. To be appreciative requires being vulnerable, but that management style is most conducive to a corporate culture of growth. When you feel their anxieties, anticipate their pains, and understand their family situations, you understand their needs and how helping them improves their lives. Trust builds, concern is returned, and the entrepreneur becomes a collaborator with every employee.

This unlocks the box. When people feel you are unreachable, they know they face limits to their self-authority, their freedom to try, their direction within the company, their ways of contributing. When an entrepreneur drops his shield, becomes vulnerable, and accepts and appreciates the humanity of his employees, he unlocks their boxes. The sky becomes the new limit, freeing employees to move and grow as fast as their ability allows them to. When this happens, the real question is whether the entrepreneur and the rest of the company can keep up.

It even heals families. Not too long ago the spouse of one of our employees contacted me regarding his wife. He took time from his

workday to call and thank me. "For what?" I started to ask. Enthusi-
astically he interrupted and said, "Since my wife joined Micrel, she
has become a different person." He went on to say that he believed
that coming to Micrel and how it changed her saved his marriage. "I
don't know what your magic sauce is," he continued, "but you ought
to bottle it and sell it."

The most important of these unboxed firecrackers are new
leaders. It doesn't matter if you have identified someone within
your company ripe for promotion or are bringing in an outside
executive for the top ranks. They all must share your vulnerability and the belief that every employee is important. When inter-
viewing outside candidates for management roles, I ask them how
they liked their previous company. If they did not like the company
and were unhappy, I see the problem being more with them. As
we established earlier, happiness comes from within. People who
are openly unhappy about their current situation probably are that
way because they are rigid in their approach and inflexible when
change is required. They may be unhappy with their boss but probably did not adapt to her style or spend enough time understanding
her needs. They may be annoyed with the corporate culture where
they work but did not assess how that culture guided the company's
mission. I look for people who were happy in their previous jobs
because they liked the challenge, knew they contributed, and only
want a bigger and better opportunity—to be let out of any box in
which they are confined.

Aside from a positive attitude, an entrepreneur should assure
that his managers embrace the corporate culture with fervor. If I
interview a management candidate, I ask questions around Micrel's
four corporate culture pillars: honesty, integrity, dignity of every
individual, and doing whatever it takes. If there is hesitation, second-
guessing, or pushback on any of them, that person would not help in

guiding Micrel. There would be a barrier between the culture and all the employees reporting to that person. Yet if managers understand those pillars, explain why they are important, and embrace them, they continuously amplify the culture. Since corporate culture must be reinforced on a regular basis, everybody in the management hierarchy must be fully vested in that culture.

The primary poisons to happiness and productivity are worry and distraction. Every human has both. Some worries are small, such as the reasonable concern for a child's happiness and safety at a daycare center. Others are as traumatic as grieving over a terminally ill parent. Distractions can come from big issues such as incompatible work assignments or smaller ones such as remembering to pick up dry cleaning on the way home from work. Worries and distractions can seem endless. They also prevent employees from accomplishing their work goals and developing their perception of value, from achieving happiness.

Much has been done in management thinking over the last few decades about this, with recognition that providing some services to employees that mitigate worry and distraction helps them be happier and in turn improves corporate performance. Yet as with any theory, some companies try to do it on the cheap and see no results whereas others break the bank and create their own class of dependents: people who expect and then demand free services as part of their employment.

From a humanistic and management perspective, alleviating worry and distraction is a good idea but wanton spending never is. Providing a dry-cleaning pickup and drop-off service is fine, but giving it away to hundreds or thousands of employees diverts money from business opportunities and the tools to achieve them. Collaborating with other local companies to establish a daycare center in an office park that operates at a cost borne by the employees who use it eases parental worries but doesn't slow down R&D by reducing its budget. It is impossible to eliminate all employee distraction and worry, and it would be nonsensical to try. A company cannot be involved in every employee's personal issues every hour of every day. Thankfully, making a happy workplace doesn't require such deep involvement or the provision of stress-reducing services for free.

Even if these services were a magic elixir for increasing employee happiness, not every company can afford them or even invest the time necessary to arrange for such services. Entrepreneurs and their start-ups may need to acquire and retain 20 key people but cannot afford to provide dry cleaning and baby-sitting for a company of 20 people. An endless string of Silicon Valley start-ups have attracted and retained key people without these benefits, which indicates that though such services may be of value, they are not the key to employee happiness. All companies, especially start-ups, thrive when employees have work that is meaningful, uplifting, and edifying. Employees gain focus when they feel value in performing that work. An atmosphere and culture that allows them to be productive and creative works even in the absence of caretaking perks.

The middle ground is to be helpful, not beneficent. A company can greatly reduce worry and distractions by helping employees find and obtain services they need or want. Micrel does have a dry-cleaning capability for employees, but it is a service that picks up the clothing at the office, brings it back, and bills the employees. We subsidize the cost, but it isn't a free service. We do not provide baby-sitting on site, but we have located and vetted places nearby where employees can get quality daycare. The wellness programs that we coordinate help employees be physically fit and psychologically better because when your body is working well, you tend to be happier and better focused. Because we understand employees' needs, we help them fulfill those needs, but we don't provide for all wants and desires.

Of course, paying for services that reduce distraction costs employees money, and money is one motivator. But it isn't the grand motivational tool that some people believe it is. I know men, working cowboys, who have never made good money, live in trailers, and drive ancient pickup trucks in constant need of repair, and they are some of the happiest people in this world. Their day begins as the sun crests over mountaintops and the only sounds are the cry of hawks in the sky and the gentle mooing of cows. They saddle their horses and ride fence lines, breathing the freshest air and drinking the cleanest mountain water. They are spiritually connected to the land, the cycle of life, and their work. They are happier than nearly everybody in Silicon Valley yet don't have enough pocket change for a second cup of coffee.

This is not to say that money cannot be incentivizing. Financial rewards do work for people who think outside the box, who are goal-driven, and who can connect achievement with success. Many employees are not goal-driven, and for them financial incentives don't work all that well. Financial incentives really help a company grow when the incentives are connected primarily to team success: the outcomes of a division or the entire company. It is insufficient to attach an employee's financial rewards to a highly personalized MBO laundry list if that list does not reflect outcomes that drive toward the common mission. Telling a programmer he'll get a bonus check if he creates 10 percent more lines of code is meaningless if the company fails to deliver a software product and thus loses money.

When you tie financial incentives to specific company goals, such as increasing revenue, increasing profitability, and cutting costs, two interesting things happen. First, each employee becomes vested in achieving that outcome and finds creative ways of doing so. The employees also become collaborative change agents, working both proactively and reactively with other employees in driving toward the mission. Tell a company that there needs to be a 10 percent reduction in costs during a year, and not only will all the employees find ways to be frugal, they will work within their departments to trim expenses and call on the carpet anyone who appears to be spending unwisely. Entrepreneurs should tie incentives to both the company and the employee: to actual corporate objectives, not a set of simplified personal outcomes.

The tough part is that most employees dislike incentives tied to company or even division goals because they feel the outcome is out of their control. More accurately, in-the-box employees dislike these incentives because they cannot see outside their own boxes and explore how the goals can be met via creativity and collaboration. This problem is not confined to any particular rank. Micrel once offered an executive a sizable stock option that was tied directly to the growth of the company. He did not like that goal because he felt he had insufficient control over how to reach it because of extenuating circumstances outside his group. Stock options for him were not an incentive because he could not find a way to make the right things happen, making him the wrong man for that particular job.

The worst of all financial incentives are restricted stock units (RSUs), also known as golden handcuffs: incentives that provide employees with free stock if they remain with the company for a certain amount of time. RSUs exist only to keep people in the company. As the former Soviet Union proved, trying to keep unhappy people in rarely works and tends only to breed more unhappiness. This means that RSUs have the perverse effect of changing people from happy and engaged employees who are focused on doing great work into silently enduring drones waiting out the clock. I suspect that the cost of nurturing such unhappiness is far greater than the cost of the stock. Because RSUs are not associated with the success of the company, there is no incentive for the newly unhappy employees to work toward any goal other than longevity, much less employ creative thinking to solve complex problems. RSUs may reduce costly employee turnover and by doing so mask why the turnover was high to begin with.

In larger companies with different operating units, establishing companywide financial incentives can be complicated or even impossible. If the goals are not fair across the company, financial incentives can become destructive. When it is easier for one group than for another to get its incentive bonus, cross-functional relationships will break down as the inequity becomes obvious. Because of this, financial incentives need to be generalized at the corporate level. If the company does well, every employee does well (intrinsic to this is assuring that each employee knows what the goals are and that the management chain helps each worker devise ways of contributing toward that goal).

Whereas restricted stock units provide the wrong type of incentive, discount stock purchase plans and profit-sharing programs are in a general way better alternatives. When employees have the option to buy shares at a discount, they have an incentive to grow the value of the shares. Their money is at risk, and they know their financial future is tied to their contribution. If their efforts produce results, not only is their sense of value (and hence their level of human happiness) raised, so too are their financial fortunes. Similarly, a more profitable company makes the sharing of those profits an exciting proposition to which every employee can contribute through cost containment or revenue enhancement. If the company does well, the employees do well across the board, not just executives with stock option portfolios.

We know that happiness comes from proving to oneself that one has value. We also see that money does not in and of itself provide happiness, but it can align people on a mission. This is where so many entrepreneurs have gone wrong, assuming that shoveling more and more money toward employees will produce a desired result when in fact it can create detrimental behaviors. Money is essential. You have to be competitive, and thus you have to spend to attract and retain talent. But since money is merely a tool for alleviating drudgery and enhancing survival, at some point more money does little extra good. Once every employee has achieved the lowest levels of Maslow's hierarchy of needs, more money ceases to have its original benefit. All new employee happiness then comes from achievement, the recognition of that accomplishment, and the culture that empowers employees to triumph.

The question is what they will achieve.

Micrel had a customer with a specific need that lit up some of our engineers. We completed the product design for that customer, but I knew and said to our product team that the project was not going to fly. I gave them my list of reasons, and they gave me a lot of pushback. They were excited about the project, clearly thinking outside the box concerning the engineering and implementation, and were almost salivating at the opportunity. Our engineering team believed it was going to be a good product. They were adamant about that.

There is always a chance that an entrepreneur is wrong. The cost of failure for this product was not insignificant but not ruinous either. I decided to let them find out since it was possible that I was wrong. Well, it turned out to be terrible, and it was very costly. It was a bad decision, which the team eventually admitted. They presented a recovery plan that involved taking the guts of that product and creating a completely new product from it. It looks like that one is going to work well and that the recovery plan was smart.

One tough discipline entrepreneurs will learn involves controlling employees while not controlling them. You need out-of-the-box thinkers who are willing to take risks, but you cannot survive with teams running in random directions with poor objectives and reckless spending. Entrepreneurs need to foster independence, free thinking, and exploration yet maintain control over product, spending, and cash.

Where many entrepreneurs err is taking the word *control* as an absolute, much as government takes the word *regulate* to mean micromanage. As a company grows, not only can an entrepreneur not control everything, but doing so would crush innovation and outside-the-box thinking. Instead, an entrepreneur's control is defined as a set of statistical bounds: determining upper and lower operational limits for the functions of the company. An R&D group may set boundaries for market saturation and profit margins before designing new products. Operations sets margins for lead times and quality. Finance has boundaries for cash, debt, and liquidity. Entrepreneurs set these limits as the means for establishing control without eliminating employee self-direction.

Entrepreneurial control becomes a method of establishing and monitoring these limits and then advertising boundaries while not controlling everything the employees do. The boundaries themselves become small points of achievement for employees, the proof of value, and the core of human happiness. It may strike some people as odd that humans could obtain happiness by meeting goals for minimum days of inventory, but it happens when their achievements are recognized.

The common thread in making people feel important is that they must sense their own value. By establishing goals, facilitating their ability to accomplish those goals, setting the boundaries to monitor success, creating a culture that encourages creative thinking, and otherwise letting employees use their inventive genius to solve problems, entrepreneurs succeed by *allowing their employees to succeed*. When employees sense that their contribution was real, that the outcomes were good, and that they were given the freedom to make great things happen, they are indeed important.

LESSONS

- Pay attention to the fundamentals of human happiness to attract and keep great employees.
- Truly happy people have found value in their existence. The primary poisons to happiness and productivity are worry and distraction.
- A leader makes people feel important because the mission he or she is on is of great consequence, and by following that leader, people create value in themselves.
- Employees are like buckets; entrepreneurs fill those buckets and keep other people from punching holes in them.
- Mutually assured happiness causes employees to fill the other person's bucket, not just their own.
- Creating a sense of humanistic support within a company begins with hiring. Finding employees who fit is better than trying to force fit employees into a company.
- Don't hire good people and then ignore them. It is like bringing a puppy home and not feeding it.
- Viewing all decent humans in the world as important because they are adding value will cause you to nurture employees differently and better.
- Leadership is the business of people, and no rigid policy can accommodate every personal situation.
- Entrepreneurs learn to control employees while not controlling them. Out-of-the-box thinkers take risks, but you cannot survive random directions, poor objectives, and reckless spending.

- Entrepreneurs succeed by allowing their employees to succeed.
- Much of Silicon Valley equates money with happiness, and thus a lot of start-ups fail.
- Financial success requires building solid cultures that increase employee happiness, and that takes time.

CHAPTER 7

Processes, Policies, and Procedures

Xerox is responsible for a Micrel policy because it shook our business pretty badly.

Xerox was in its heyday. It was the master of many imaging industries and at that moment in time was a significant player in printers. It did very well and was leading the market with its innovations. Xerox was coming out with a color printer, which in that era was a market innovation.

Micrel wanted a piece of that business. Because we believed Xerox and its position were rock-solid, Micrel developed the power management parts for that printer. Our engineers put a lot of time and effort into inventing the products we sold to Xerox and, as a much smaller company back in the early 1990s, banked big on Xerox as its printer went into production. This one product represented almost 25 percent of Micrel's revenue. With Xerox's market presence and power and the projected sales for the printer, Micrel stood to make a small killing and grow rapidly.

I got a call from Xerox's purchasing department letting me know that they were going to cancel the project, that Xerox was not going to build that color printer or use our chips.

Though public announcement of that decision mildly signaled the start of Xerox's decline, it was a cannonball to Micrel's hull. We had already geared up to deliver. Our engineers had to put other projects on hold, our manufacturing had tooled for large production runs, and everybody in Micrel was focused on little else. I braced myself to run that part of Micrel's business on an international scale, with inventories and everything else in place to meet Xerox's expected demand. Instantly, we lost almost a fourth of our business. It was a traumatic moment, and we had to move quickly. I couldn't wait a week or two; I had to shift gears immediately. Unfortunately, we had to let some good employees go, a painful process I do not enjoy. We had to tell vendors that we no longer could accept certain orders.

This is why Micrel has a policy that we will not bank our business on any single product that accounts for more than 20 percent of our revenue stream. Though a 20 percent cut is hard to deal with, a 25 percent drop is dangerously close to catastrophic. Other semiconductor companies have evaporated by losing that much revenue without being ready for the impact.

This is one of the many values to thinking through and enacting your corporate policies and procedures from experience. Our experience with Xerox birthed a policy to prevent potential catastrophe that was triggered twice again. Micrel had contracts with both Motorola and Lexmark, and I specifically limited our exposure to a maximum of 20 percent of our revenue. In both cases, when Motorola and Lexmark's internal business decisions caused them to stop buying from Micrel, we survived the blow with far less impact than there was during the Xerox episode.

Such policy and procedure decisions are important and come with their own trade-offs. For example, we eventually lost Lexmark as a customer because we would not risk selling it chips that would make Lexmark account for more than 20 percent of our business. Micrel also may have missed some bottle rocket–type growth by not rolling the dice with other huge contracts. But the lesson learned from partnering with Xerox was that it is better to grow rationally, albeit more slowly, than to die as so many other Silicon Valley semiconductor companies have by betting big and losing even bigger.

One of the tough things entrepreneurs need to learn to love is writing policies and procedures. It is a big mountain to start climbing when you first hire people and a task that becomes ongoing. It's not something that you just sit down one evening and do. There are lots of policies and procedures across every part of a company and for thousands of issues. For creative entrepreneurs, writing policies and procedures is an unlovable task they must learn to love because in the long run policies and procedures prevent disasters, scale an organization, and free up the CEO's time.

When Micrel started hiring its first employees, I began working late drafting our first policies and procedures. Most entrepreneurs begin with human resources policies because they are the first critical ones that must exist for employees to be treated equitably. You have to deal with vacations, holidays, time off, and issues of that nature.

No one likes to write policies and procedures, but I had an unfair advantage: I was fortunate enough to acquire copies of policies and procedures from other companies that were willing to share theirs. After reviewing them all and finding the strong commonalities among them, I crafted my own from those templates. Maybe other people are unfortunate enough not to have such prototypes and are forced to think through all situations and decide what a smart policy for each one is. However, start-ups don't have the luxury of time, and cloning other companies' policies and procedures is a faster and more economical approach because those policies and procedures have been tested to some degree.

It has been said that simple and clear principles give rise to complex and intelligent thinking, whereas complex rules and regulations give rise to simple and stupid thinking. Then again, too few rules invite anarchy and chaos. This is where many entrepreneurs develop ulcers.

There is a basic dichotomy between the creative and passionate drive of the entrepreneur and the stilted bureaucratic necessity of policies and procedures. One seems diametrically opposed to the other. Many Silicon Valley start-ups crashed because their founders thought that hiring smart people would magically bring order out of chaos, that everyone would do the obviously "right" things. The problem is that people are individuals. Each has his own history, his own set of ethics, and his own priorities. Without policies and procedures, those individual inclinations can pull an organization in every direction except the one an entrepreneur wishes it to go. As boring and uncreative as policies and procedures look, they are one of the foremost tough things that an entrepreneur must learn to love doing.

Simple and clear principles, the underpinnings of both corporate culture and company policies and procedures, rely on the KISS principle: keep it short, stupid (or keep it short and simple for gentler minds). Complexity brings its own version of chaos, namely, the chaos of inaction. One need only look at the world's largest bureaucracy—the U.S. federal government—to see that when things get overly complex, they also get stupid. The more complex an organization makes policy or procedure, the more opportunity there is for confusion, mistakes, rework, or inaction resulting from fear of bureaucratic reprisal. Governments have created such complex mazes of regulations that most of what constitutes government work involves understanding the regulations and asking for more and more clarification.

Conversely, many great Silicon Valley companies—even global enterprises employing tens of thousands of employees—operate on simple cultural policies and procedure guidelines. This makes the mission and the vision for accomplishing the mission easy to understand, easy to enculturate all employees with, and easy to let all the employees know where they fit within that framework. It gives the organization flexibility while mitigating the risk of many hands and minds working simultaneously. Complex policies and procedures that make employees wonder if they should be sitting or standing will eventually make them walk out the door.

The more complex you make a process or a procedure, the more likely it is that it will never be implemented. Incidentally, the same principle applies to communications when one is trying to express a point to an employee. Basing your conversation on an immediate issue and providing feedback with simple guidelines allows the employees to see how your mission applies to them. Issue a long diatribe, a lecture, and a litany of prescribed comments and you will lose the employees' attention and commitment.

So why have policies and procedures in general? Bureaucracy exists to keep people from doing dumb things. Policies and procedures provide the minimum amount of necessary bureaucracy. Policies and procedures codify human principles, such as establishing an equitable vacation policy across the company. Policies and procedures can also bolster the corporate mission by narrowing the latitude employees have in pursuing opportunities. Policies and procedures are a primary means for ensuring organization health by preventing obvious bad habits.

If you hire the right people, they tend not to make dumb mistakes. But everybody is fallible, and so principle-based policies and procedures become like locks on a door, which are designed to keep honest people honest (any competent burglar can break into any house or office he chooses regardless of the number of locks on the door). Dishonest people will violate your policies and procedures just as they might willfully disobey public law. Policies and procedures are guidelines to create uniformity of action throughout an organization. Simple, principle-based policy that is plainly presented is rarely violated.

One hazard occurs when your policies and procedures are too different from those of the rest of your industry. When you hire people from other companies, there is the risk of their not understanding the new policy and relying on what they understood at previous jobs. It may even be unintentional, as one midlevel manager confessed: "Well, that's not the way we did it at our old company. I guess I just had the habit of doing it that way."

In Micrel's early days, it never dawned on me that we would be terribly different, but some of our policies and procedures were different enough to cause a few bumps along the road. It is smart to review the policies and procedures in concert with normal or standard practices throughout your industry rather than trying to come up with some clever new policy that risks being uncommon. The reason for this is that when policies and procedures are too clever or are unique to your company, they often aren't followed. Since people tend to remember only 10 percent of what they studied or learned, many of your written policies and procedures may be forgotten, and employees will fall back to the policies and procedures they knew in other organizations or resort to common wisdom.

Micrel was once tossed a curveball concerning merit increases calculated on a curve. At Micrel, our annual merit reviews are based on a list of characteristics that we use to measure each employee. We do not score on a curve. Instead we award merit for merit, for how an employee performed. Yet just as some college professors grade their students, other companies grade on the curve. They rate employees on the basis of who is the best and who is not the best and then skew all the scores in between. We hired a manager who came from such an environment and scored his team accordingly, which made his staff look overly competent compared with the entire company.

This didn't sit well with other managers and employees. Policy must be uniform when it comes to how people feel as a part of the organization. As a leader, as a CEO, any specific policy you create with regard to reviewing employees, measuring their contributions, and establishing the relationship between the company and the employees had better be uniform. Different divisions and departments can diverge in regard to time off, national holidays, and work from home. But if they differ on the basics, such as what constitutes performance worthy of a salary increase, you must ensure that your managers understand the letter of the policy to be carried out.

Policies and procedures become more important as a company grows. A company without an organizationwide vacation policy would default to time-off schedules decided by each department or even each manager. Interdepartmental operations would probably grind to a halt as specific groups were less available than others, and resentment between departments would grow as one or another group received more time off. Corporatewide policies on receiving gifts may matter most to one group, such as a purchasing department, but must be applied to everyone to prevent sources of undue external influence (Micrel's gift-receiving policy forbids any gift with more than nominal value; anything over that has to be reported to management or refused).

Such policies and procedures mainly look after the long-term effects (any policy that tries to manage short-term transient issues is simply unworkable). In Micrel's 37 years, there has not been a single instance of the company being helped when an employee violated a policy or procedure. There may be a temporary benefit to the company, but the long-term effects would have been worse.

For example, an employee once obtained a component at a very low price, which was very beneficial to the company. But it came at a high cost because he was more or less dishonest and had cheated the vendor, which dinged our reputation with that supplier. We corrected the problem and resumed a good working relationship with the vendor, but that violation of Micrel policies and procedures did us no lasting good.

It isn't natural for entrepreneurs to love policies and procedures, but it is essential. They learn to love this unlovable task mainly by seeing their policies and procedures work. Micrel has a policy that disallows the use of belittling language. Employees who embrace this policy soon see the benefits for themselves and for Micrel. They notice that they never hear anyone talking down to them, which makes working at Micrel less stressful than working at other companies. They see how people are more willing to engage one another and thus are openly collaborative. Employees who don't buy into this policy tend not to last long either because we ask them to go or because they cannot function without being antagonistic.

Over the years, I have enjoyed watching this policy more than most, and its success made the unlovable task of setting policies and procedures a pleasure. To see an entire company abandon a negative trait and for the results to be a happier and more productive workplace was an accomplishment worth striving for.

Finding the balance between policies, procedures, and progress is part of the entrepreneurial craft. There is an inherent conflict between policies and procedures and nurturing empowered employees who are creative and largely independent and think outside the box. Policies should exist to channel their daily efforts but not constrict them. Finding the balance is important; otherwise your company goes nowhere as a result of inaction or unguided effort.

Policies are guidelines. The local department of transportation doesn't force you to drive in the exact middle of your lane, which would be impossible. Instead, it paints guidelines on the roadways to channel thousands of vehicles into a general path. Corporate policies and procedures need similar mild constraints, pointing the way down the highway of business.

Strict policies and procedures have the same perverse effect as too much government regulation, which has strangled certain industries into stagnancy. When employees are uncertain whether they can or cannot turn right or left because they may be in jeopardy of violating policy, they'll be frustrated to the point of finding employment elsewhere. Policies and procedures composed as guidelines are much more likely to be understood and obeyed. More important, guideline-level policies and procedures lead to the complex thinking that entrepreneurs need on their team and that helps build thinking organizations.

If you make the rules too complex, you eliminate thinking. When one's work life is about reading manuals and doing nothing more than what is allowed, no actual thinking is required (and such jobs are abandoned by thinking people). Complexity leads to nothing more than compliance. However, guidelines that reflect principles require employees to examine how to achieve corporate objectives, which requires creativity. The more flexible or general the policy or procedure is, the more thinking is required and the more creative employees must be.

The downside is that if you make policies and procedures too nebulous, the human instinct to seek the path of least resistance takes hold or the creative thinkers' visionary capabilities may establish outsized schemes. Either way, indifferent or nonspecific policies and procedures create the wrong effect, as happened once with managers importing their own policies.

I ran into a problem in which Micrel had a policy with regard to a particular job function. A new executive came to work for us and imported the policies that were in force at his old company and were distinctly not Micrel's. Unchecked, his imported policies took over and became the standard because they had been implemented. After a while I noticed changes in the way part of Micrel was operating.

"Why were you doing it that way?" I asked someone up the management hierarchy once I had a handle on the fact that the policy had changed. "Well, because that's the way you've always done it."

"That may be the way we've always done it, but only since your new teammate came on board." Because Micrel's policy was perhaps a bit too fluid at the time, a new policy was established and the employees thereafter just followed historical practice; they never examined what was the written policy or procedure. As in watching the financial operating metrics, an entrepreneur needs to monitor her teams for policies and procedures compliance issues. You must constantly ping your team and consistently reinforce the company's procedures or create new sets. Otherwise unofficial policies and procedures will appear to rise from the muck and, left unchallenged, can become the de facto standard.

Simple and principle-based policies and procedures balance potential conflicts between independently thinking employees and the inherent need for interdependence between teams. After all, every employee is aligned to accomplish a known mission, yet each is allegedly empowered to pursue that mission with a great deal of flexibility. Companywide policies and procedures provide guidelines that make one follow the other. Rigid and complex policies and procedures lead to the attitude that "that's company policy, and that is all

I will do," whereas vague policies generate an attitude of "I'll do this my way!" Policies and procedures as guidelines become policies that unite employees in their approaches to working with one another.

This cannot be done in a vacuum. You must constantly polish policies and procedures by refining them as well as assuring that they are being followed. Policies and procedures abandoned by employees may have weaknesses, but more typically the policies you fail to monitor may cause institutionalized abandonment, a case in which a policy that is not being enforced is then assumed to not be in force and is ignored. Like most companies, Micrel has an audit department that tracks the various functions of the company and measures whether the policies are being followed across the board. A by-product of this effort is the modification of those policies to bring them up to date with current business conditions.

A common mission and vision and the policies to drive them create interdependence of thought, which helps employees think together. Without policies, building cross-functional relationships is more difficult. Policies and procedures should create guidelines for good relationships between departments and encourage them to work together. In the absence of policies and procedures, departments can create silos that may not be intended to create working barriers but do. Unchecked, everybody eventually sticks to her own silo. An entrepreneur is constantly breaking down silos and fostering intercompany skills and interdisciplinary relationships. Policies and procedures accelerate this by eliminating conflict between departments or between people in different departments. Micrel's weekly operations meetings are used in part to review and generate policies and procedures that work toward various objectives and goals of the company. Getting departmental managers to discuss their challenges often reveals problems with policies and procedures or the way they are implemented to one or another department's detriment.

Collectively talking about cross-functional issues puts policy and procedure issues out in the open, and the problems find rapid solutions.

Why this works is a clue to entrepreneurial management. When people in their different departments see the benefit of cross-functional relationships, they seek reasons to work together. Instead of feeling that policy is increasing their workload, they avoid shifting responsibly to other departments and instead examine the policies that lead to conflict or to work barriers. When teams have the ability to examine the modes and guidelines of the way they work together, their joint creativity improves.

I once intentionally decided to launch a product that required all three Micrel business units—our analog, timing, and local area network groups—to work together on the project. Because the groups were aligned on a single mission, they functioned as a collective unit, and I was seeing some of the best working relationships ever. In doing so, they had to craft policies and procedures that drove joint product development, and as a by-product they created policies that are now facilitating better collaboration for all products.

As this bit of Micrel history shows, leadership and the more boring policies and procedures work that an active CEO must do are not mutually exclusive. Whereas leadership is often mistakenly thought of as charisma, employees more clearly see the entrepreneur's vision, mission, and goals through policies and procedures. They are the standards by which the company will operate whether they are customer, vendor, or employee policies. This clarity gives all the employees an understanding of who they are as part of the organization and what they all are trying to accomplish and how. It goes well beyond employees, though they are the first and primary beneficiaries of clear policies and procedures. Many of Micrel's policies are published on our website so that people seeking employment understand the organization before applying. Micrel business standards are also published on the web so that our customers and vendors know our policies and understand how those policies direct our relationships with them. In an environment based on honesty and dignity, not publishing these policies and procedures can lead people to suspect an organization's motives or methods.

New entrepreneurs should embrace policies and procedures early. Policies and procedures allow an entrepreneur to safely hand over control of routine corporate functions to his employees and as a by-product allow him to focus more on his vision. We have all seen the workaholic, the person so focused on her job that she forgets about her family and even her personal health. Humans have to find balance in life, and entrepreneurs need to find a balance between strategic issues and process. Policies and procedures define recurring process-level functions without hands-on involvement, giving back to the entrepreneur the time and attention needed to lead.

Policies without principles do not work. Stripped down to the core, policies are a reflection of the corporate culture and by proxy of the entrepreneur. They are the written rules of behavior to achieve goals within the culture. Happily, culture eliminates the need for complex policies and procedures. If you have a culture of honesty and integrity, you do not need to cover every single aspect of employee behavior. Google famously said, and I paraphrase, "Don't be evil," which guided its employees away from some profitable but unsavory opportunities in digital ad sales. When you hire the right people and provide them with simple, principle-based guidelines, they will govern themselves. In Micrel's 37-year history, I've never encountered an employee who said, "I didn't know that was against the policy of the company." Principles must be the foundation atop which policies and procedures are written; otherwise they are useless.

This can give some entrepreneurs heartburn when the policies and procedures don't work and are not followed. Either the guiding principles are wrong or the policy doesn't reflect the principles. It takes a fair bit of soul-searching to determine whether the principles are wrong because they are the entrepreneur's, his institutionalized ethos, his heart. If the principles are wrong, the entrepreneur needs to accept that there may be something wrong with his outlook on life and business. Alternatively, his principles may be perfect but perfectly ill-suited for his industry. Or there may be a great match between his principles and his markets, but the policies and procedures are written in such a way that they do not accurately reflect those values. Whatever policies and procedures you draft, ensure that they match the principles of you, your company, and your industry.

Defining those principles and documenting them in succinct ways makes writing the subsequent policies and procedures much easier. Micrel holds to the basic tenets of honesty, integrity, the dignity of every individual, and doing whatever it takes. These four principles are spelled out in such a way that no employee can mistake who we are, and they document what we believe. When writing policies and procedures, we review these four principles and ask ourselves if the new policies and procedures adhere to them, if the scope and the intention of a particular policy are aligned with our values. The extensions to these core principles are then easy to understand. Does a policy treat everybody fairly? Does it apply equally interdepartmentally and outside the company? Does the policy single out any particular group, team, department, or foreign office? Does it in any way favor one or another gender, sexual orientation, race, or religion? Is the policy suitable across the board?

Fairness is a critical factor in creating policies and procedures. It doesn't matter how sage and beneficent your principles are if they are not applied equally. Policies and procedures that fail to respect the integrity of every individual with regard to local background and personhood will cause a policy to be reviled by an employee somewhere. At Micrel, our employees reflect most of the world's religions. Some practice their faith in ways that require different times off, which we accommodate. We provide flexibility in such matters because they are important to the person, and it would be dismissive to set time-away policies strictly for the convenience of one creed or another or one country over others. Calendars for Seventh-Day Adventists, Jews, Muslims, and Catholics are not going to align. Since denying people the ability to obey the tenets of their faith would be disrespectful, our policies and procedures strive to accommodate them within reasonable bounds.

In the early days of any company, all policies and procedures are companywide policies and procedures. It is easy enough to create policies and procedures for a handful or even a couple of dozen employees. But once different groups form—different departments, different divisions, remote offices, and the like—policy and procedure development must be delegated. At this point corporatewide policies become the domain of the executive team, which sets the guidelines for what policies and procedures can and should be managed at lower levels. If you don't have company standard policies and procedures in place, it is hard to develop departmental procedures and still adhere to the principles of the company.

Policies and procedures are important throughout the company, but they are absolutely critical in specific areas. Any policy or procedure that deals with employees has to be written, vetted, debated, and revised. Employees are people, and policies that affect people affect our fellow humans, their families, and their futures. It may be tedious to write an employee handbook and define the details concerning merit increases, time off, sick days, vacation, and terminations, but leading people without their understanding the rules within the organization would be impossible. Focus on human resource policies first because you deal with your employees first and daily. You work with employees long before you can even talk with your customers or vendors.

Next are the people outside your company: your vendors and customers. They need to understand your rules for honest dealings, whether this involves return policies or long-term supplier contracts. Published terms and conditions that are consistent are more likely to be accepted by your vendors and customers. You will quickly learn if your terms and conditions are onerous, because vendors and customers will refuse to do business with you. Like employees, they want more than anything to be treated fairly and with respect, and publishing your policies is a show of openness and honesty. Similarly, your quality standards are important to know, to keep consistent, and to document in the open. Letting buyers and sellers understand how you measure quality, how you handle customer returns, and what corrective action you are willing to take communicates a willingness to do business in a way that mitigates risk.

To a creative, out-of-the-box-thinking entrepreneur, writing policies and procedures sounds dreadful. Learning to love policies and procedures seems impossible on the surface, and waiting years to witness the results offers entrepreneurs little incentive to roll up their sleeves and create concise policies. What can make this tough task enjoyable from the start is the art of coordination.

Watch a well-trained gymnast at work. Every muscle has been trained to achieve what it needs to do. Every tiny fiber has an effect on the gymnast's total performance. However, the discipline that allows his deltoids to hold an iron cross is vastly different from the training his big toe received in providing balance and direction in vaulting onto a pommel horse. His body is strong through generalized discipline and exercise, but it is coordinated through rather specialized conditioning.

Creating corporatewide policies and procedures and establishing processes for the development and tracking of departmental practices is the art of coordinating the body of the company. Like a gymnast's arms, legs, hands, and feet, each department will have its own individual policies and procedures that govern operations within its particular groups. Just as a gymnast's overall physical conditioning coordinates his body, a company's procedures and policies govern how intercompany or interdepartmental relationships are coordinated. A corporate policy may describe how employees are treated on elements common to all people, but departmental policies and procedures may dictate the actions of specific job functions. Corporate policy may describe how to handle expenses, but R&D department policy describes what engineers may spend money on.

Policies and procedures should be as minimal as possible, especially when it comes to cross-functional operations within the company. Departments and divisions have a difficult enough time collaborating across organization boundaries, and a good deal of the entrepreneur's time is invested in opening channels of communication between them. Erecting rigid policies and procedures that hinder interdepartmental interaction may be necessary but should be streamlined. Purchasing affects all organizations, and so does planning. If policies and procedures are too restrictive in the pursuit of protecting the company from uncontrolled spending, this could freeze necessary spending. Like many companies, Micrel has a central purchasing department and is careful about ensuring that purchasing policies are uniform. This does not mean that every department has the same purchasing regimen but that purchasing policy equally affects all of the organization and does not particularly hinder one group or another.

Employees will tell you soon enough if policies and procedures have become too detailed and too restrictive. It may not be delivered as a blunt statement but in the form of inaction. Either productive work slows as people tire of combing through policy and procedure manuals or the employees simply stop paying attention to policy to get work done. It may also manifest itself in complaining about why the right things are not happening. When this occurs, you need to look at why, backtracking from the specific policy violations and work stoppages to the policies that caused them. You may have to review a departmental policy and, if it is not in error, then look at corporate policy. If the policies are not abusive, the very underlying principles may be at fault. But examine them you must because neither reaction—the slowing of work or open disregard for policy—leads to healthy outcomes.

It is best to review policies and procedures before they are published and not afterward, and they should be reviewed not only by the people directly implementing a policy but by people outside the policy's direct influence. At the top levels of an organization, the board of directors may well review corporate-level policies after the CEO and departmental managers have had their several and joint review sessions. Policy developed for one department should at a minimum be reviewed by the head of any other department that works closely with the originating group and by departments that have organizational oversight (e.g., if a department policy involves compensation and benefits, human resources is always engaged).

LESSONS

- Entrepreneurs need to learn to love writing policies and procedures. It isn't natural, but it is essential.
- Simple and clear principles, the underpinnings of both corporate culture and company policies and procedures, rely on the KISS principle: keep it simple, stupid.

- Many great Silicon Valley companies operate with simple cultural and policy guidelines, making the mission and the vision easy to understand and easy to enculturate.
- Bureaucracy exists to keep people from doing dumb things. Policies and procedures provide the minimum amount of necessary bureaucracy.
- Policies and procedures mainly look after the long-term effects; any policy that tries to manage short-term, transient issues is simply unworkable.
- If you make the rules too complex, you eliminate thinking. If policies and procedures are too nebulous, human instinct seeks the path of least resistance or creative employees may establish outsized schemes.
- When people in different departments see the benefit of cross-functional relationships, they seek reasons to work together.
- Employees will tell you soon enough if policies and procedures have become too detailed and too restrictive. It may not be delivered as a blunt statement but in the form of inaction.

CHAPTER 8

Finance and Finances

I t was a 1954 Ford coupe.

Like many men on campus, I had a love affair with my car that might have rivaled those I had with coeds. And though a Ford coupe was not prime muscle car material, I spent hours and all my money trying to convert it into a road monster. What I discovered is that although my love for cars is enduring, my love for *that* car was only temporarily endearing.

Like many youngsters, I failed to fully understand the expense of automobile ownership. Before the coupe entered my world, a bicycle got me around as needed. But bikes lacked the masculine panache of owning a car. An automobile offered the ability to take me wherever I wanted to go whenever I wanted to go there. Distance, rain, stamina, and image were all limiting factors to a college student on a bike. When the chance to buy the coupe came, I didn't even think about what it would cost in gas, repairs, insurance, oil changes, enhancements, and repairing those add-on enhancements that took the poor old coupe beyond its specifications. Despite my souping it up, it never ran for beans. Swapping the automatic transmission for a manual was time- and income-draining and ultimately bad for the vehicle. My bank account soon dwindled to zero.

But I didn't think about the expense, just about driving my not so hot rod.

I soon was selling some of my valuables just to keep my car going. I hocked my trusty rifle, some of my fashionable clothing, and other things that I cherished just to keep my car on the road. My coupe was making a wreck of me. It hurt because I was constantly trying to raise money to fix the car. I finally depleted my cash, and Dad said, "Just park it." There I was, literally stuck. I couldn't get back on my bike again; it just didn't seem right to peddle after expending so much effort, money, and pride on the coupe. I struggled to think of ways to finance the vehicle because my aspirations for wanting the car exceeded my logic. It seemed like every dime, everything I earned was going into that car. As my bank account bottomed out, so did the palatability of my driving privilege.

This is pretty much the way Silicon Valley operates.

The difference between what is *endearing* and what is *enduring* is much like the difference between a lover and a spouse. Your intents are very different between a dalliance and marriage. An entrepreneur can spend his energy creating a product that like all products has only a limited life span, or he can build a company that adapts and grows. Products are endearing like short-term flirtations, but building a business that outlasts you is an enduring endeavor.

That is why working with venture capitalists is like souping-up a 1954 Ford coupe. An entrepreneur's focus becomes less on designing a company, building a culture, and creating an enterprise and more on the next funding round. Because first-round investors are product-focused and want a fast return on their investment, the entrepreneur becomes defocused on building his business and engrossed with finding money to continue operations and grow rapidly regardless of how endangering both activities are to the company. Every day he spends looking for the next funding round is a day when he has not thought about broader product lines, deeper services, or a culture that creates self-sufficient employees. The money hunt keeps entrepreneurs from constructing their businesses and achieving their missions.

Silicon Valley exhibited an ugly pursuit of endearing products during the dot-com explosion. It was somewhat understandable because nobody knew what commercialization of the Internet would look like, and so venture capitalists tossed money at every entrepreneur with roughed-in code and something akin to a business plan. As companies launched big and the revenues failed to materialize, their CEOs spent all their time hunting for more investor cash. With the CEOs on the money hunt and away from attending to their companies, these new businesses never received the guidance needed to rationally grow and soon enough died when the money ran out: no revenues, no margins, and no taste for additional risk on the part of venture capitalists. It still happens today, though VCs have become a bit more circumspect.

However, they remain impatient, and that impatience perpetuates the money hunt that poisons many promising entrepreneurs.

The common question posed to entrepreneurs when VCs ask for a huge hunk of a start-up is: "Do you want to be rich or do you want to be king?" The two are not mutually exclusive. You can get rich if you are lucky, have good market timing, use VC money to propel early success, and exit via acquisitions. But the odds are against you. Silicon Valley venture capitalists are happy if 1 in 10 of their investments pays off, but from a business success standpoint, that is a lousy batting average. This explains why VCs' profitability is typically quite low: their payoffs are infrequent, and they lose quite a bit of capital.

Micrel recently acquired a venture-backed company. We bought out the VCs for less than $8 million after the venture capitalists had invested over $70 million in the company—nearly 10 times what they pulled out of it. For 11 years the company's various CEOs (yes, multiple heart transplants had been performed on this infant enterprise) worried about investment money, and for 11 years VCs fed them enough to keep going in the hope that each CEO had time left in his day to build a company.

Micrel had a much different history because I wasn't looking to become rich, though that did happen. I wanted to run a company, which by default made me a king. I didn't necessarily care about being rich, though the consequences of being a start-up king made it more likely. The difference was intent. I wanted to create an enduring company, and wealth was merely an artifact of doing so. When I founded Micrel, when I made myself the organizational leader, I didn't wear a metaphorical golden coronet studded with diamonds and jewels; it was a Burger King paper crown. Unlike many VC-backed start-ups, I didn't have a fancy office, I didn't drive a fancy car, we didn't serve catered lunches, we forsook padded expense accounts, and we eschewed opulent lobbies. We rescued gear from salvage yards, repainted it, and refurbished it. We made do with junk.

And we did it on my personal credit.

Knowing that I wanted to avoid venture capital and family loans, I approached three different banks. I knew that banks didn't lend to start-ups with unproven management teams and no products. But since the alternatives—VCs and family—were unacceptable, I decided to make it work, to make the banks lend me kick-start capital.

Two banks flatly refused and in such a way that I assumed I might be escorted out of the building. But I learned enough from those encounters to plan the third attempt. That was the First

National Bank of San Jose, which later became Bank of the West, and we are still their customer today.

I sat down with two gentlemen from the loan department. Their initial response echoed that of the previous two banks. "We don't lend to start-ups" was the rather blunt assessment, though there was no indication the bank guards would be called to show me the location of the front door. "Okay," I replied. "Let's just pretend. What would it take for this bank to lend to a start-up?" I wanted to understand why banks feared lending to new tech companies and thus how I could resolve those issues.

"Well, it's not worth our time because we're not going to do it," they said. "So what's the use in pretending?"

"Because it will help me. I want to understand why banks won't consider lending to a start-up." After a bit of round-robin chatting, I sensed they wanted to appease me or get me out of the building. But they agreed to create a term sheet—a list of what a bank would require of a start-up like mine—as a way of showing me the barriers and then showing me the door. "Remember, we have no intention of lending any money to you."

I didn't hear back from them for a couple of weeks. They wouldn't answer the phone, so I walked back into the bank and asked them, "Have you prepared that document?" They said, "We'll have it for you in a couple of days," so I went home and returned two days later.

They kept their word and presented their perfectly ridiculous terms for lending an unknown start-up their depositors' money. I read over the terms, and they were very onerous. Their utterly unreal covenants included terms such as a ratio of debt to equity of 0.5 to 1, meaning I would have to put in twice as much money as I got in the loan. They also insisted that I could never lose any money at any time, even on a quarterly basis. They wanted me to be profitable from the get-go. They tossed in more covenants strictly regulating cash flow, how much cash I had to retain on hand, and so forth.

"Do you have a pen?" I asked. They looked a bit puzzled and inquired why I needed a pen while one of them reached for it. "Well, I just want to borrow a pen." They handed one to me, and I said, "Okay." I signed the document. "I'll agree to this." This group of otherwise stoic bankers was visibly flummoxed. I kept the pressure on them, holding up their unacceptable term sheet. "Here's your offer, and I'm accepting it."

"Wait a minute," they practically stuttered in unison. "This is not an offer. You just said to prepare a document."

"This is a formal offer you're making me. I can see it, and I agree to the terms."

"Why would you agree to this? You won't succeed. You'll fail!"

"Why would you want me to fail?"

"Well, Mr. Zinn, we don't want you to fail."

"Then let's make some of these terms more reasonable."

It was about at this point that they knew they had been had. We started negotiating back and forth with regard to the covenants; I managed to get them to relinquish some of the more ridiculous ones. The required debt-to-equity ratio became 1 to 1 instead of a 0.5 to 1. We found common ground regarding cash retention at the bank and corporate profitability.

"How about if I'm profitable on an annual basis as opposed to a quarterly basis?" They said no. I nudged them a bit more. "How about two quarters of profitability?" They said no again. "You got to give me at least something." One of the bankers countered, "We'll give you one quarter where you can be unprofitable, one quarter out of four." I got a sinking feeling in my stomach because it is very difficult for a start-up to be profitable even on a quarterly basis much less to hit its numbers in three out of four quarters. But that is what we agreed to.

A bemused banker leaned in and said, "This is the first time in the history of this bank that we've ever loaned to a company that really has never been in business. Has never been an ongoing success."

"Good. I like to be the first. Not only that, but I want you not only to loan me the money, but I also want you to finance this piece of equipment, and I want to be 100 percent financed, including the taxes." They looked at me as if I had something growing out of my head.

"You got to put something down on it," the formerly genial banker replied.

"I'm already putting up half of the cash. You're going to loan me $300,000, and I'm going to put up $300,000. I need something for working capital because of your strict covenants." They finally agreed to finance 100 percent of the equipment that I was buying if for no other reason than that it was usable collateral. But it was an important term because this piece of equipment was basically the guts of my new company. I had to modify my business plan and the business I was going to go into to support a monthly loan payment, but I made it work. I was able to secure some testing services work from other companies, and the company was profitable from day 1. It would have been impossible to start out as a full-blown semiconductor company making deliverable products. I had to begin operations by doing services for other companies.

In the end, my bluff paid off in several ways. Much of the bank financing was covered by equipment collateral, and that reduced some of my risk. But being the most affluent of the partners, the bank was in effect relying strictly on me to pay off the debt if the business went bust. I was collateralized six ways from Sunday, which provided me plenty of motivation to make Micrel instantly and consistently profitable.

About six years later, after Micrel was doing quite well, the bank came to me and asked if I'd like to get off the guarantee, to no longer be personally responsible for the debts of the company. I knew why they offered me the chance to escape: it was expensive for the bank to keep renewing the paperwork every year when it was obvious that Micrel would pay off the loans.

I told them that I wanted to think about it.

That stunned them. "Why? You should want to get off the guarantee."

"Well, that depends. The culture of the company is to be profitable and to do whatever it takes. I like the feel, that edge, that keeping my nose to the grindstone. I get that when I know my home is on the line. Not only that, but I can tell my people, my employees, that I'm on the hook for the entire debt. It keeps them loyal to me."

A week later I followed up with them and let them know I was staying on as a guarantor. "That's a first," said my contact at the bank. "We never, ever heard of anybody wanting to stay on a personal guarantee when they easily could've gotten off of it."

Everything I owned was on the line. Everything. Every asset I had. Since no bank lends 100 percent of the value of your collateral, I had to hock it all to launch Micrel: the house, the family cars. I even pledged savings and stocks. It was the best of alternatives. Taking money from family has many possible and unpleasant complications, and since family is more important than anything else, it seemed unwise to jeopardize familial relationships. VCs would want control, the one thing I did not want to surrender. Crowdfunding did not exist as we know it today. Therefore, I headed to the bank, offered up my entire personal worth, scripted covenants the bank could not ignore, and landed the equivalent of $900,000 in today's dollars.

Debt financing has motivational as well as enduring benefits. First, you can lose your business only if you fail at being profitable.

Financing with banks is like floating a mortgage on a home, whereas taking VC money is like a reverse mortgage, in which somebody else owns your house. Having your assets on the line with bank financing drives you to find ways of being immediately profitable, which Micrel was in the first year. Though nobody likes paying interest on bank loans, the interest I paid to launch Micrel was far less than the value of the stock I would have surrendered to VCs. It also gave me the control I needed to create a profitable company as opposed to one that unprofitably grows market share rapidly as well as one that remained consistently profitable for over three decades in an industry in which competitors routinely lose large sums of money.

The discipline of putting profit first is important to enduring companies and the art of building a lasting enterprise. If you are going to start a company, you must focus on being profitable. Your home is on the line, and unprofitability may lead to street camping. If you are merely trying to get rich, you don't necessarily have to be profitable since other people's money is at stake: you simply have to ship a product, ramp up market share, and then get rid of it by selling your product vision to somebody else. Being king of an enduring business gets in the way of the VC's mission. They want you to get in and then get out, and they don't necessarily want you to be king; they want you to make *them* rich. They don't care if you become rich in the process; well and good if you do, they believe. But your wealth is at best secondary in their hierarchy of objectives, and creating an enduring business probably isn't on the list at all. VCs only try to preserve their clients' capital and gather enough wins to make their funds profitable.

Micrel didn't have a product. Sure, I had an idea for products and thoughts on how to run a new semiconductor company, but my timelines for success were much longer than most VCs would have tolerated. They were looking at a five- to seven-year exit horizon. I could have done that, but that was not the way I wanted to run the business. My goal was the creation of an enduring company that I could lead into a strong market position. I wanted a company from which I would retire on my own terms. I wanted a company that disproved the profitability fluctuations of an entire industry. From the start I knew this would take more than the five years a VC would accept.

Americans in general are an impatient people, which isn't bad. Our impatience has caused us to accomplish many spectacular things, and we have learned to do the impossible. Because of the trade-offs their clients could make with alternative investments, VCs are impatient as well. This drives a lot of entrepreneurs into believing that fast wealth is the right, and sometimes the only, way to succeed. They accept the idea that they can be king and wear the diamond-studded crown today. Faux trappings of success such as well-adorned lobbies, new manufacturing equipment, and free organic gourmet coffee make some start-up CEOs feel like successful kings without actually earning the title.

This insatiable desire to get rich and do it quickly underlies modern Silicon Valley. Some entrepreneurs are working to build global sustainable enterprises. Many are looking to exit as quickly as their VCs want. Most launch without profitability being a consideration, moving hastily toward grabbing as much market share as possible with the mistaken belief that competitors cannot work around the initial gains. Instead of focusing on customers and market mechanics and building an organization that constantly performs, they try running as fast as they can in hopes that a much larger company will pay them many multiples over their already overinflated valuations.

They believe this because it happens often enough to be believable. So too does a young athlete believe he can become an NFL star quarterback, and so too does a girl brought up singing in church believe she can become a multiplatinum pop star. The probabilities are about equal.

Impatience can be a killer if you are not focused on the long-term mission of nurturing an enduring corporation. Micrel did not start as a product company because trying to invent and engineer a product would have taken too much time to ensure first-year profitability. Instead we started as a services company, though that was not the long-term objective. This was a slow-growth plan of action, not a get-rich-quick scheme. Because we were profitable in the first year, the banks knew we were reliable and obtaining money was never a problem. The employees knew we could make it work, and so they stayed and we attracted more great minds. Customers were more willing to do business with us since they knew we would be around the next year and all the years after that. Suppliers gave us preferential pricing. Slow but profitable growth laid all the planks under Micrel's feet and made significant expansion all but assured.

Growing organically is not dissimilar to the way most Americans buy homes. I bought my first home when my wife and I married in the 1960s. We paid a little over $15,000 for it, or about $120,000 in today's dollars, which in Silicon Valley buys nothing. After a few years and children, we moved up. Later still, we upsized again. We just kept moving up. Most homeowners do that. Very few start out with large homes because the risk is too great.

Similarly, enduring companies such as Micrel can start small and move up stepwise without surrendering control. Micrel's first office was 5,000 square feet. A few years later it was 10,000, and then it went up to 20,000. It's the same principle. In the run-up to the Great Recession, home buyers broke the old pattern of buying just enough house to hold their families and instead "invested" in McMansions: opulent cookie-cutter miniature palaces. These homeowners overextended themselves and when the recession came were forced to short sell their homes back to banks. Many of the Las Vegas suburbs are littered with these microestates that you can buy for half the original price.

What impatient entrepreneurs and the venture capital investors like are fireworks. Fireworks are grand and wonderful. They look great but are designed to either explode or fizzle out. Venture-funded companies do both. Most merely sputter into nonexistence. Others blow up by blowing out, busting once a sudden shortage of cash makes them go out with a bang. A few explode into the brilliant display of color their VCs hoped for. Fireworks and firework-funded companies are fun, but they are also dangerous.

Enduring companies are not fireworks. They are hoists in garages. They lift great loads and sustain those masses for long periods. Enduring companies are rarely glamorous. They are savvy, diligent, and disciplined, and they grow wisely. They sustain arsenals for long periods. They are not vivid, colorful, or even exciting, but they last.

If you believe enough in your business and your acumen in running it, there are many different ways in which you can fund your company. Avoiding conventional wisdom about funding may show you paths that make more sense. When I launched Micrel, numerous people told me it was impossible to kick-start a semiconductor company making integrated circuits (IC) while being profitable on an annual basis. They say this even today. But Micrel proved them wrong. This happened in no small part because we took a different funding path in which we arranged covenants with the bank that required that we be profitable at the end of the year. That being imperative, we kept our costs down, started small in services, and found efficiencies others overlooked. Aside from one year with a small loss in the wake of the dot-com implosion, we have always been profitable.

Not that getting bank funding was a cakewalk. Banks do not like lending money to start-ups. The failure rate for start-ups is high, new management teams don't have track records, and it costs more to start a semiconductor company than to start a corner deli. When I walked in the bank's door, I already had the outline of a pretty clever business plan. I knew in advance what they might ask for to get me to go away, and my business plan showed how I would deliver. Since banks make more money the longer you borrow it, they would be happy if it took me years to repay the debt as long as payments were made on time and Micrel's profitability was steady.

Even though people in your industry, VCs, and even conventional wisdom say that you cannot run a company profitably from the start, it simply isn't true. Profitability is a matter of discipline, not running before you walk. It takes a different kind of acumen—one with structure, patience, and discipline—to be willing to do it with less, take a little longer, and constantly explore options and alternatives for every job. If you train your business mind and then choose a way to launch and grow your business, it ought to be and can be cash-positive from the start. If you feel that the business you have in mind cannot run properly from day 1, consider not going into that business or be willing to surrender a great deal of equity to get funded.

Regardless of where an entrepreneur gets the start-up cash, managing it is all-important. People do not go out of business if they have cash. The issue then becomes the management of money, the control of spending, the incentives for revenue generation, and the anticipation of times when revenues do not meet the business plan. Most start-ups that fail do so because of cash. They spend money recklessly, their revenue predictions are irrational, or they don't bank enough cash to float operations during transient dry spells. The first two situations involve entrepreneurial discipline: being realistic and managing spending to accommodate true needs and true revenues. The last one, banking cash for business climate fluctuations, is where too many entrepreneurs allow aggressive growth to overtake their reason.

No industry, economy, or business is perfectly predictable. Micrel has been consistently profitable, but we have had revenue ebbs and flows. To make payroll, you have to make sure you can weather temporary changes in your business climate. You always want to have at least one quarter's worth of excess cash to fund your operation. If your company is doing $4 million a year, you should make sure to have at least $1 million in cash to fund operations. If you can't hold at least a quarter's worth of cash to fund your company, you don't really have an ongoing operation.

Cash gets ever more important if your business plan involves running a deficit for some period. In those situations it is the combination of operational expenses and anticipated shortfalls that defines the amount of cash to have on hand. If a start-up will lose $1 million and has an operational budget of $1 million, it needs $2 million just to keep its nose above water. Some entrepreneurs do not segregate their margin loss from their operational expenses. These blurred lines lead to faulty cash management projections. They think they are running their companies well enough by watching quarterly numbers but end up surprised when consecutive quarterly expenses and deficits are combined. Enterprises suckled on VC money keep spending, keep running out of cash, and perpetually restart the money hunt instead of perfecting the organization and product line.

Often this bad situation results from being overly excited about their growth potential. Note that they see *potential*, not *results*. By viewing the company's potential, entrepreneurs can become blind to downsides and how long it takes to get their operations into a profitable mode. They tend to underestimate how long it takes them to become successful. According to the Census Bureau's 2012 "Survey of Construction," the average new single-family home takes seven months to build from obtaining a building permit to driving the last nail. People outside the building trades tend to think it should take only a month or two. If they attempted building their own home and being their own general contractor, they would probably not bank enough cash to complete the job. Many new general contractors fail because they think they can build faster and cheaper than is possible and run out of operating cash before a client's project is complete.

If you think that your business is going to take a year to get off the ground, you need to assume that it's going to take two to three years. Your funding needs to stretch that entire three years and not be based on the possibility of early profitability. If you do it in one year, if you deliver ahead of realistic expectations, everybody will be happy, especially your investors. On the flip side, if you are overly optimistic, you will burn through available cash and collapse, and nobody will be happy. Most Silicon Valley start-ups are way too optimistic, and that inflames the money hunt problem. Venture capitalists like optimistic stories and impassioned entrepreneurs. This leads to speculative VC funding, encourages poor fiscal management, causes the entrepreneur to seek more venture capital, and so on and so on until the founders have no equity and their invention is sold off to the highest bidder.

This may be the actual intent of some VCs.

I don't think venture capitalists intentionally want their portfolio companies to have bad fiscal discipline. VCs usually have somebody from their organization sitting on the board of the companies in which they invest, helping to manage their progress. But actively participating VCs do not assist in creating enduring companies because they have little interest in them. Their guidance is not on realistic cash management to internally facilitate paced, steady profitable growth. Between rosy projections and VC encouragement, poor cash management in funded start-ups is much more probable. Because nothing in life ever goes according to plan, running a start-up on a fast track with poor cash management leads to cash shortages and the CEO rejoining the money hunt. Before long, either the entrepreneur or the venture capitalist is forced out of the cycle. One or the other walks away, and it is typically the one with the money bags.

Hitting those unrealistic growth numbers leads to other poor management practices. The company resorts to lowering product selling prices in hopes of grabbing market share even though most marketing strategists will tell you that this leads to a damaged brand reputation, which in turn diminishes sales over the long run. This leads to average selling price blindness, poor gross margins, and changing expectations about burn and loss rates. Their hopes soon devolve into the belief that they can scale into profitability. "Sure, we lose money on each deal, but we make it up in volume." Sometimes their companies do grow volume, but the market saturates, new competitors find ways of stopping growth, and new technologies make current ones obsolete. In all these cases, the entrepreneur never banked cash, ran out of it, and his company was effectively auctioned off for dimes on the dollar.

An entrepreneur should keep in mind that though venture capitalists are investors, they are also gamblers. They play the odds. That is why if 1 in 10 of their investments pays off, they believe they did well. Because so few investments pan out, their risk is huge. *Forbes* once reported (http://www.forbes.com/sites/timworstall/2012/04/23/does-venture-capital-actually-make-any-money/) that after the dot-com bust, VCs had an average beta of well over 1, which means that venture capitalist risk was more than that of an index fund (from a risk perspective, their limited partners would probably make more money betting on the same stodgy stuff on which middle-income Americans wager). Since 1999, as a group and with notable exceptions, VCs have not been very profitable. A recent Kauffman report shows that the typical venture fund didn't return capital to investors after fees were taken out, that only 20 percent of these funds generated returns higher than the S&P 500, and that a full 62 percent of them underperformed the public stock markets.

A VC who invests in your company is gambling. Unlike Vegas blackjack victims, they are making informed gambles, but it is still a gamble because they see potential that can be fulfilled only with irrational growth and a handy exit. But some similarities are striking. Both the blackjack player and the VC know they are going to lose a few hands and win a few others, and so they are trying to improve their win rates. Both the blackjack player and the venture capitalist tend to raise their bets on perceived trends and hunches. And for both, any day they walk away from the table with a tiny bit more than they came in with is a good day. The only difference is that when the venture capitalist raises his bet, it is the entrepreneur who folds by giving away more of her company.

When VCs do win, they win big, and this is the source of insanity in Silicon Valley. Sometimes winning big means covering the other nine losses, and sometimes it means Google or Facebook. Without the big wins, the numbers never work out and the venture funds close, leaving limited partners to wonder why they too did not "get hit by the money truck." This explains why so few venture capital firms make a reasonable return on their investments, why they underperform aggregate stock market funds. It isn't because they don't understand business (though a few do not) or because they don't understand markets. It is because they are placing a large number of bets on many companies and are willing to sell off any portfolio company that didn't hit it big.

If a venture capitalist says, "I'll take a bet on your company," he means it quite literally.

Though I avoided venture capital in forming Micrel, VC gambling has helped change the world and Silicon Valley. As in the music business, there is a lot of talent that would never be known to the public unless someone had gambled on those artists' success. Sam Phillips gambled on both Elvis and Johnny Cash, and the world of music changed forever. Silicon Valley benefited from venture capitalists because they were willing to place bets in general and occasionally big bets on key technologies.

But I also wonder how Silicon Valley might look today if more companies had decided to grow organically and more slowly. The culture would be radically different, based on establishing great corporate cultures that employees embrace, such as Google, Apple, and Micrel. More companies that had great ideas might still be around as opposed to having burned through their investor cash before fading away. Silicon Valley would attract people who want to create empires instead of exit strategies.

The most important decision an entrepreneur must make early on is whether she is a gambler. If she is, taking venture capital, running as hard and as fast as possible, and constantly being on the money hunt can pay off despite the fact that the overall track record for this approach is not terribly good, at least by VC profitability standards. The other approach is to start with as little funding as possible, grow more slowly, spend frugally, expand gracefully, and treat your own cash as the bank on which you will always rely. One way you would be a sprinter, the other way a marathon runner.

The difference is financial conditioning, making cash king instead of the CEO. Financial burnout occurs in companies that lack such conditioning, amplified by the flabby reasoning that there will always be another VC round and another cash infusion. Marathoners who do not condition themselves never reach the finish line, or at least not the same day in which the race started. Running an enduring company, one that rapidly becomes self-sufficient and is designed to be around forever, is like running a marathon: you and the company must be conditioned. A conditioned entrepreneur knows cash flow pitfalls and is aware that many, many things can go awry. These entrepreneurs don't run their cash flow close to the edge. They don't spend on unnecessary things. They monitor cash as carefully as—perhaps more carefully than—R&D efforts. They acquire savvy advisors with cash management experience. They train themselves to endure the grueling long-distance run.

Unreasonable expectations and unrealistic projections tend to drag entrepreneurs away from running a marathon—building an enduring company—and toward the VC mode of making nonathletes run sprints and hoping they get across the finish line first. This is exacerbated by the conflict between the entrepreneur's passion and patience. A passionate person will take great risks, enter dangerous territory, and gamble with his own life to reach his goal. A patient person examines the terrain and plots a course for the next step, not the other end of the field. She makes it to her goal on a slower, more gradual schedule. Entrepreneurs like this ask, Where should I go next from here? Can I run again tomorrow as opposed to next year? They view business as a journey, not an event.

Fast growth and the poor cash management that too often accompanies it are what cause many entrepreneurs to kill their own companies. Entrepreneurial passion causes them to expand too quickly because they see a fleeting opportunity and run after it. Micrel could have raised more in venture money than in bank financing and started with new silicon chip fabrication facilities and all the trappings of a company ready to run. We could have engineered products from the first day. And like many long-forgotten semiconductor companies, we might well have vanished. Our mission was always to become a semiconductor manufacturer, but we started life more modestly. We could have burned through three years of VC money before releasing our first product, but instead we lived on our own cash and were under nobody's control. We could have tried to rocket to instant success but instead decided to be around forever and create a company that could do that.

Growing too fast often means you are running out of money more quickly. It's just like running a race. When you start off too quickly, sprinting from the starting blocks, you will run out of gas too soon. You won't finish the race. Managing cash in your business is akin to pacing yourself during a long-distance run. You set up financial objectives on a short time frame with long-term objectives, just as a runner would set a mental objective of running only the next mile as opposed to all 26 miles of a marathon at once. You watch cash numbers quarter by quarter. You set rational milestones for what the company will accomplish within that period. Only when you meet those milestones do you consider speeding up, investing more of your cash, and striving for more market share. In contrast, if those milestones are not met, if your company fell short of objectives, you avoid investing in more growth because there is something wrong with your projections, your management, or your market. If you do not understand what you did wrong in the first quarter, speeding ahead almost assures that you will fail in the second quarter too.

The model, goals, and cash management criteria that you set for your company are not static; believing that they are is an endangering blindness. Entrepreneurs should constantly monitor the success of their business plan and vigorously argue all assumptions within the underlying models. Micrel runs to several models: gross margin model, operating model, operating margin model, and more. Each quarter we review how the model matches the as-run data and make corrections. We pay attention to how this affects cash and the survivability of the company and have worked this way from the start. Aside from the willingness to do whatever it takes to be a success in the market, this constant review and refinement has been the foundation of our nearly perfect profitability record.

"You'd be a tough guy to starve out because you keep your money in a cigar box," said a good friend of mine, a local mogul in the commercial real estate business. "You hand your money out one dollar at a time."

It has never been quite *that* frugal at Micrel, but we do not easily tolerate wasteful spending. It is not overly dramatic to say that poor cash management in a corporation leads to human suffering. It can be as mild as no Christmas bonus check and as harsh as layoffs or as deadly as bankruptcy. If a company fails to manage its cash, fails to hand it out in metered and monitored ways, at some point there will not be enough cash to sustain nominal operations. When an entrepreneur watches spending, when he approves expenditures and makes sure that each expense is consistent with his budget and is applied to the corporate mission, cash crunches become rare. When a company begins life with an entrepreneur with this mindset, the positive frugality to proactively manage cash becomes part of the corporate culture. Employees will avoid submitting expenses that are inconsistent with wise spending and driving toward the common corporate mission.

Annual planning broken into quarterly objectives is the best planning cycle, especially in volatile industries such as high tech. Entrepreneurs should measure company performance against the quarterly plan and watch how the annual plan will be affected. Critical to the cash-is-king mentality is controlling spending within each quarter, increasing spending only out of necessity and when revenues justify doing so. The spend rate for each quarter is compared with the cash on hand, and if available cash does not cover at least two quarters of operations, spending must be reined in.

One quarter does not a trend make. Two quarters barely show a trajectory and constitute the minimum planning revision cycle. When you manage to a two-quarter measurement phase, you see definitive trends, not just transient blips. When two quarters in a row show that revenue is growing, an entrepreneur can be comfortable increasing expenses. Conversely, if revenues are not growing or if, heaven forbid, they are shrinking, the entrepreneur needs to cut expenses in order to stay on her plan. That is a painfully difficult thing for many entrepreneurs to do—to cut back. Being optimistic types, entrepreneurs tend to mislead themselves by saying, "This is going to turn around any minute! Revenues will go up."

But that isn't life. Projections can be wrong, and markets can be unyielding. Faith, which is defined as belief without proof, is fine for religion but a disaster for revenue planning. Faith in rising revenues leads to faith that spending will not be a problem. Together they lead to cash shortfalls, missed payrolls, and possibly financial failure. Make sure that you're spending to your budget, that spending does not expand until you have had at least two quarters in a row of revenue increases.

One interesting side effect of frugality and consistent spending planning is that employees are happier to work for you. This goes against the perception that elegant offices and perks make employees happy. Hardly a week goes by, even in good times, when one or another company doesn't announce layoffs. Sadly, downsizing has become a financial management tool that compensates for poor cash management. Layoffs hurt real humans. They make meeting family budgets painful, they cancel vacations, and they postpone college. Headcount reductions are rough on real people, and poorly managing expenses is a poor excuse when families and their children are affected. Employees who know beyond any real doubt that their jobs are secure because their company wisely manages expenses have the single largest worry removed from their lives. They can focus not on fretting over how to make ends meet but on self-actualization, their growth as people both within and outside the company.

Micrel has been in business for 37 years and has been consistently profitable. Because of this, Micrel has very low employee turnover.

Frugality alone isn't sufficient. Micrel is more consistent than even larger companies in the semiconductor business, and some of those other companies are quite frugal. You can tell by looking at the bottom line in their quarterly statements; the more profitable they are percentagewise, the more frugally they probably are run. Micrel remains one of the best in the industry; we are known for how well we are managed. But we don't suffer the radical ups and downs of some of our competitors. We avoid layoffs. We remain consistently profitable while other companies can lose millions of dollars in a single quarter.

Such performance requires patience. In an impatient world, in a fast-moving industry, patience may seem like the wrong quality for a founder to have. But patience in this case applies to the entrepreneur's long-term mission and the management of finances to achieve that objective. When a company has a good product and a sound business plan and is not trying to grow too quickly, patience and discipline lower the probability of calamity and help everyone in the company focus on the company's goals. Being patient and letting the business build itself with its own cash is preferable to building it on a false pretense. Try building a skyscraper on landfill rather than on bedrock and you will see the analogy to cash. The skyscraper built on a landfill will not survive a strong breeze, much less one of Silicon Valley's routine earthquakes. Finding bedrock land, drilling or blasting to create pylon supports, and adding seismic architectural components takes more time than rapidly erecting the same skyscraper on silt and grit. It will also ensure that the building is there tomorrow. It will weather almost any storm.

Growing a business internally by using your own cash to expand is cheap. Borrowing is unavoidable, and at the very least a good line of credit is necessary to work through unexpected situations. But your cash costs you nothing, and it even earns a little interest until it is used. Borrowing costs a little, but giving away equity costs a lot. A patient entrepreneur who manages corporate cash and expenses can grow the company in a consistent and inexpensive way.

The one perverse effect of frugality as a corporate norm is that sometimes employees are intimidated by spending or even use the pretext of cost to avoid doing what they do not want to do. Since I drive Micrel's culture, including its "cigar box" spending habits, to this day I hear people say, "He won't approve that," and they will not even ask if an expense is wise and allowable. This can create problems when people have real needs and great ideas but believe that the subject is not worth discussing because it will be rejected automatically. Similarly, some employees, especially middle managers, might use the excuse "He won't approve that expense" to kill projects or initiatives that they do not want to do. A frugal reputation is great, but a tightfisted one has downsides. One thing is for certain, though: if you're not frugal at the top, your employees won't be either. Spendthrift CEOs encourage employees to waste money in very creative ways.

Entrepreneurs need to watch for cultural changes that indicate the organization is losing its frugal mindset. When expenses approach revenues, it is more likely to be due to increased spending than to reduced income. With the knowledge that there will be spending exceptions, namely, for capital expenditures, outlays should be about equal to or marginally lower than revenue. This shows you are spending within revenue boundaries, and if those expenses are not frivolous, they should be contributing to corporate growth to the maximum rational extent.

If you walk around your facilities—and you should daily—you may see things that are out of place, contrary to a frugal spending philosophy. Often these decisions of lower-level managers need to be checked before they become the new norm in terms of what is an allowable expense. If you see free coffee in one department, expensed employee lunches in another, and free baby-sitting services in a remote division, these are visible signs that middle managers are not part of the thrift culture. Every dime devoted to unnecessary expenses is a dime not devoted to necessary ones.

Ponder your development cycle and your time to market criteria. For most companies, there are seemingly never enough resources to get products designed and shipped to beat competitors. Would more resources have helped? Would hiring another engineer speed the testing cycle? Would an equipment upgrade improve product quality and gain market share? Is free coffee worth forgoing those other needs? And if not those needs, what about the hundreds of lesser but still important needs throughout the organization?

No company thrives without spending money, and so the goal is to prioritize spending, to make wise investments. Foremost is product, which in turn means everything required to design, build, and service the product. Next is marketing, for no product sells itself. After that comes operational efficiencies and back-office needs. Nowhere on the list are elaborate lobbies, mahogany offices, corporate airplanes, company cars for the whole executive team (all too typically a fleet of luxury sedans and town cars), off-site junkets to the Ritz, most hiring bonuses, and lavish expense accounts. Many CEOs have the latter, spending tens of thousands of dollars on posh restaurants and private limos. As the longest-serving CEO in Silicon Valley, I probably charge Micrel less than a thousand a year, whereas some CEOs I know spend a thousand a week. After more than 10 years as Micrel's CEO and once the company was well established, I finally arranged for a company car for myself as part of my compensation package, in part because my base salary is below the industry average. Every dollar I don't spend on myself goes to making Micrel profitable and our employees more secure and to improve our position in the market.

In Silicon Valley and the other tech hubs around the world, there are a lot of really bright entrepreneurs who lack financial acumen. They may be great leaders and can perform calculus equations in their heads, yet they can't balance a checkbook or craft a coherent revenue projection model. Entrepreneurs need to surround themselves with smart people, and that includes smart mentors. On all matters financial, the smarter the mentor, the better.

Mentors and great board members are necessary external sanity checkers. If they are recruited from your industry and related synergistic industries, they can provide valuable control over poor cash management and improper forecasting. If you don't know how to run a company, what are you doing running one without expert guidance? Some entrepreneurs rightly believe in their technical abilities but wrongly believe in their managerial (in)abilities. They all too typically underestimate the discipline required to run a company and the mechanics of fiscal management.

Trust and competency in your business are codependent aspects of good financial advisors. It is not enough for a financial advisor to understand finance. He should be intimate with the nature of your industry and help anticipate how cash will ebb and flow with industry-specific changes. He will know how to help establish budgets and monitor the results. Imagine that you were in a car accident, were rushed to the hospital, and are connected to an array of medical diagnostic machinery. Those monitors will not help your healing if your doctor doesn't understand the metrics they report or the boundaries that mark your vital signs as being outside a normal range. Likewise, a financial advisor from a completely different industry may not understand all the metrics important to your business, may misinterpret reports based on those metrics, and may well prescribe the wrong therapy. You want your doctor to know what a rapidly falling heart rate means in the context of your injuries and your medications, and you want a financial advisor to understand the pitfalls that your industry faces and what changing inventory levels and sliding margins mean to your business.

Policies and procedures can be useful in molding fiscal discipline throughout an organization, but the effectiveness of policies and procedures depends on what kind of business you are running. Basic business models tend to track revenues and expenses as covariant financial items, and controlling spending should follow revenue projections. Some industries, especially ones with long lead times from investment to revenues, cannot model directly on a quarter-to-quarter basis. Oddly, many in the social media industries are in the basic model camp but treat investing in their companies as if they were manufacturing concerns and commit to heavy up-front spending on the assumption that there will be a timely revenue return.

Watching your competitors' financial models will tell you if your forecasting and spending are reasonable, though there is no need to mimic any particular industry average. But it is an important tool for watching your spend rate and perhaps seeing when a competitor is not properly managing its rate, thus creating a market advantage for your company or a warning that your competitors are investing for new products and markets. Part of your operational financial plan should be to say, "Here is how my competitors run their companies. Are the ways we differ an indicator of something important?" Monitor their operating and gross margins as well as changes in their spending and then make sure you are not too far outside the mean.

A tricky part of fiscal planning involves product strategy. Investing in certain products and market sectors can be expensive, and if the strategy does not pay off as projected, you can encounter a cash crunch. In one of Micrel's few errors, we ventured into the consumer products market, making chips for various devices. We soon discovered what we had not recognized about consumer electronics, namely, that the semiconductor market in that market is like being on powerful narcotics: once you get on it, it's hard to get off.

The consumer electronics market moves fast, is highly fickle, and has amazingly swift margin degradation. By the time you engineer a semiconductor product, the entire market segment you were trying to serve may have radically changed or even disappeared. Yet those markets are addictive because they require billions of chips for a single product. At its peak, Nokia shipped 200 million units of just one mobile phone model in a year. Today that Nokia doesn't exist.

For a while, Micrel chased that dragon, enjoying the thrill of fast-moving development and the chance to churn out billions of chips for people around the planet. But because the markets are as lucrative as they are transient, many competitors are constantly entering and leaving, with many of them going bankrupt in the process. Prices plummet and margins dwindle quickly. Failing to factor in rapid price erosion is what killed many chip companies and even dinged Micrel. This was a case in which Micrel and its advisors were not intimate with the market they were serving and did not forecast revenues according to the faster price erosion in consumer electronics semiconductors. The result of rapid price and margin shrinkage is that revenues don't grow even as sales volume increases. Consumer electronics chip companies enter a hamster wheel of addiction, jumping rapidly from project to project, market segment to market segment, chasing the high of being the first into a segment that has the potential for explosive growth and exiting once everybody else has entered the segment. Micrel found that the average selling prices of our products dropped faster than we could reduce costs to compensate.

That was an expensive investment in Micrel in terms of capital, in terms of personnel, in terms of employee frustration, and in terms of lost opportunity. We had to reorganize or reorchestrate our design efforts, refocusing on industrial, wireline communications, and enterprise/cloud infrastructure spaces. That took a complete change in mindset because it also required us to slow our growth. It was a painful decision because pivoting an established company increases operating expenses as the product lines are redirected into other markets, which means spending more while earning less. A company with poor fiscal discipline and wasteful spending habits would never survive such a transition, but Micrel maintained good profitability while doing it.

Perhaps the bigger mistake was that the consumer markets went against part of Micrel's culture. We purposely grew at a slower pace throughout our history for a reason: we wanted to be consistently profitable. Entering the consumer silicon markets changed the dynamics. The industrial end markets we now profitably enjoy tend to be slower growing, but they have higher margins and little of the pricing volatility we encountered in consumer markets. We enjoy more consistent profitability because of the strategic decision not to be a consumer chip addict.

An artist friend of mine is fond of saying that the masters knew how to paint over their mistakes. In business you will never make the right decision 100 percent of the time, especially on products to take to market. But as with a painter, it is not the mistakes you make but how you recover from them.

A .38-caliber revolver taught me a bit about correcting mistakes.

I was 15 years old and, having grown up on a ranch, knew my way around firearms. I once came upon a revolver stuck underneath some clothes in my dad's closet. Though I had shot many rifles, handguns were still a novelty to me and I thought this particular revolver was pretty cool. Like many youngsters who watched Western movies of that era, I wanted to see what kind of quick draw artist I could be. I went into my mother's bathroom, aimed at myself in her mirror, and squeezed the trigger.

The unloaded gun was not as unloaded as I thought.

The blast in that confined space was deafening. The bullet smashed my mother's dressing mirror and the medicine cabinet and went through both the cabinet and the backing wall while shattering most of my mother's cosmetics. The bullet flew down the thankfully unoccupied hallway and embedded itself in a lathed and stuccoed wall.

After a short but stunned assessment, I realized what I had done and knew I had a choice: either correct my mistake or face some more serious consequences. I opted for the former. Dad was coming home in a matter of hours, and since he used the newly shattered mirror to shave in the morning, I started by replacing that mirror. This proved to be relatively easy, taking only a couple of hours after I found the correct size mirror glass. Luckily, my mother was going to be gone for a week while traveling to San Diego, and so I had time to address the rest of the damage. After reading the labels on her cosmetics, I replaced each of them. I later patched and painted the hole in the back of her wooden medicine cabinet.

But the bullet did damage to the far hallway wall that would be obvious to anyone, so I also needed to quickly patch that. The biggest problem was finding a paint that matched the ugly green hue in the hallway without having to repaint the entire wall. Thankfully, the bullet did not exit the wall on the other side; there was no actual hole, but the surface was cracked and it was easy to see. I was able to effect all the repairs and paint jobs in less than three days, and all these years later no one in my family is the wiser (though they will know when they read this book). Aside from learning that a gun is always loaded regardless of what one thinks, I learned that we all make mistakes, but it is how we correct our mistakes that matters.

Sometimes mistakes lead to improvements. My mother thought her eyesight had improved because she could see herself better in the new mirror. Of course, I chuckled when I heard this.

Sometimes financial mistakes are minor, such as having imperfect revenue projections that lead to minor cash crunches. Sometimes they are big, such as banking your future on one big buyer who vanishes and leaves you with nearly no revenues. Regardless of the mistake, you must change direction, whether it is a relatively pain-free belt-tightening on spending or a major corporate product realignment. To keep gambling on the same failed course is to put desire ahead of data, and that is deadly.

Knowing and having some control over the variables of revenue and costs is important to fiscal management and business decisions. When you are uncertain of your degree of control, caution is advised because the costs can be large. Micrel had a foreign customer that lost its market and as a result defaulted on a contract. We decided to file a lawsuit to get the money owed us and thus meet our financial plan. But law and lawyers are always outside your control, and the situation is compounded with international law. An old joke claims that a lawyer is someone who defends your interest and takes the principal, and like many jokes, it is based in truth. We spent a tremendous amount of money litigating only to lose because little of the issue was in Micrel's control. You can't help being a defendant in litigation, but when you become a plaintiff you willingly put your fate in the hands of judges and juries, none of whom have your specific interest at heart.

Financing and financial management all revolve around risk balancing, and this includes both personal risk and company risk. When you are starting your company, the risks are all personal, and as you grow, they become corporate. Mitigating risk, whether by deciding how to fund your start-up or figuring out how to plan billions in cash flow, comes down to understanding the risks involved and handling them correctly.

When you are starting your company, one option is borrowing. Some people have launched by taking money from friends and family, but I don't recommend doing that. These people are more valuable than anything else you encounter in life, and money creates contention, especially if you stumble and cannot repay the debt. The risk involves the very people you love who will otherwise support you in times of crisis. This is never worth risking.

Bank financing, as I did when launching Micrel, risks your personal assets and credit. Vegas gamblers have a motto: never take to the table more than you are willing to lose. When you put personal collateral on the line, you run the risk of losing it—losing your house, your car, your child's college fund. Weigh these risks carefully. Over the long term you can get another house and another car and rebuild a college fund, but time always works against you; bank financing may be a young person's gambit. But of all the financing options, no other will rivet your attention to the details of running your business more than knowing that the bank can evict you from your home.

Thanks to the Internet and the phenomenon of crowdfunding, you can raise significant sums of money from a lot of people with no serious risk aside from back-end payoffs that often are copies of the product you plan on selling anyway, which in turn may help create product buzz. For product-focused entrepreneurs with low initial capital needs, this is the best of all options provided that you have a product people deeply desire and the media savvy to pitch it well.

If your capital costs are high, there may be no alternative to venture capital. The risk with VCs is losing control of your destiny. They want to be king in order to get rich, and controlling your company is important to them. In first-round investments you may give away as little as 10 percent of your company, but if you need multiple cash infusions, you may sacrifice 90 percent. Once VCs have 51 percent, you are no longer in control of your destiny, much less your company. It is in their interest to eventually get that magical 51 percent. If you have plans to slowly grow an enduring company, they will replace you with someone who will attempt to engineer rapid growth and a tidy exit.

How you finance your company is a case of control or be controlled, and that entails understanding both your risk preferences and your business goals. Companies that are product-strategic have a small time window to grow market share, which fits well with a VC's ROI window, typically five to seven years. If you have an endearing product and want to make a chunk of money and then leave it to an acquiring company to convert the product into something else, giving limited equity to a venture capitalist is not a terrible option. If you want to be Steven Jobs and create a company and culture that people love and remember, it is a horrible choice.

Even in my industry, the silicon chip business, we see divergence between endearing companies and enduring companies. In the 1980s both Linear Technology and Maxim launched but did so with company-strategic objectives. They entered markets with lines of products atop which they could build out into related fields. They had a vision for a company, not just a point solution. Atheros, in contrast, was a company that had a Wi-Fi product and was recently sold to Qualcomm. They were an endearing product-oriented organization.

If the realities of venture investing and endearing products are not vivid enough, think for a moment about the popular *Shark Tank* series. None of the VCs at the table there want to run a company; they already have their own enterprises to worry about. Instead, they want to benefit from your product idea. Offer a 10-year payback on a long-term corporate vision to Daymond John and you won't get a penny. But show off a product concept with a much shorter window, one with exit ROI in the first years, and you'll get his interest.

The other aspect to finances is controlling yourself and, through being a personal example and through policies and procedures, controlling your costs. There is a reason that the year 2000 is recalled as the *dot-bomb*. A period of irrational expectations overrode the sensibilities of investors and entrepreneurs alike. Silicon Valley's fiscal excess took every possible manifestation, from gold rush market share grabs (such as Webvan) to venture capitalists investing in nothing more than a vague idea (Boo.com, which burned through $135 million of venture capital in less than 18 months). Hiring bonuses included company-paid leases on BMWs. No employee bought his or her own lunch. Companies spent millions to put sock puppets on television during Super Bowl games. There was no restraint.

Why did that happen? Why did the venture capitalists not ride herd on their portfolio companies? Why did people believe that the cash well was bottomless? Why was there this excess of spending?

It was because faith and greed overtook reality, and venture capital money helped complete the illusion. There was a belief that a new era was coming online. In anticipation of a fundamental change in the way people communicated, miles of fiber cable was laid (much of it going dark soon thereafter). Nobody quite knew what the Internet would really turn out to be, and we still don't. Because of the belief that it would change everything although nobody quite knew how, venture capitalists spread their bets wide and deep. They poured cash into flimsy firms with little executive experience and even less-proven product demand. In other words, businesses grew too quickly. They weren't well managed. They weren't well controlled. Because venture capital was abundant and venture capitalists were not riding herd on their investments, there were few controls. For a time, it seemed everybody was making money and anybody who could build a web page could start a company because demand was so great.

During the bubble, Micrel was growing at a 67 percent compounded rate, as were peer companies.

That unheard of top-line growth rate was the warning sign that most other companies missed. I saw it, and I was worried. After looking at the numbers, seeing where the cash flow problems were, and watching the strain of venture capital funds that had exhausted their pools, I forecast the dot-com implosion about a year before it happened. I could see that the growth rate was unsustainable. Something that looks too good to be true probably is. Growth alone was not the only signal. I started to see inventory buildups in Micrel and in other tech companies. I had already started an austerity program, anticipating the downturn, when one customer called to tell us that they couldn't take a shipment of our products they ordered because they didn't have enough warehouse space left.

Seeing the storm clouds, Micrel took cover. We slowed spending. We immediately backed off on our growth plans and started digging in our heels. Sure enough, the bubble burst, and like many in the tech business, Micrel saw its revenue fall almost in half come 2001. Most companies cannot survive a 50 percent reduction in revenues. They typically cannot borrow enough to dig themselves out, and many tech companies died in the dot-bomb era. Even though Micrel lost almost half our revenue, we were still profitable in 2001 because we chose to base our financial monitoring in reality, not a belief in never-slowing markets. We chose to control our spending before the market forced us to. We got our costs down before our revenues fell.

We shrank our inventories. We didn't build as much product. Sadly, in a rare event, we cut back people, and that was mainly because I had calculated a 30 percent market retreat instead of the full 50 percent that occurred. It was painful, but not as painful as what other chip companies encountered. They suffered big losses. Many of them went out of business. We survived because we took the necessary action in advance. And that action might not have been possible had Micrel lacked a corporate culture of rational frugality. All things considered, Micrel came out of it quite nicely.

We move very quickly at Micrel. We have a saying; fast is not fast enough. But that applies to more than getting products out the door. It applies to nimble responses to changing financial conditions: monitoring cash, anticipating changes, and responding creatively and frugally. We run the books at a rapid pace so that we can remain one of the most consistently profitable companies in the valley.

LESSONS

- Silicon Valley operates largely on fleeting passions, not on creating enduring companies.
- Venture capital causes entrepreneurs to focus less on designing a company, building a culture, and creating an enterprise and more on the next funding round.
- Being king and getting rich are more mutually dependent than mutually exclusive.
- Debt financing has motivational benefits.
- The discipline of profit first is important to enduring companies and the art of building a lasting enterprise. Profitability is a matter of discipline and not running before you walk.
- Impatient entrepreneurs and venture capital investors are like fireworks. They look great but are designed to either explode or fizzle out. Enduring companies are not fireworks. They can sustain great loads for long periods.

- Enduring companies can start small and move up stepwise without surrendering control.
- People don't go out of business if they have cash. Managing it is all-important.
- Venture capitalists are investors, but they are also gamblers. They play the odds. That is why if 1 in 10 of their investments pays off, they believe they did well.
- Fast growth and the poor cash management that too often accompanies it are what cause many entrepreneurs to kill their own companies.
- Growing a business internally by using your own cash to expand is cheap. Borrowing costs a little, but giving away equity costs a lot.
- Oddly, frugality and consistent spend planning make employees happier to work for you.

CHAPTER 9

Growth Creation and Management

Asparagus grows very fast, yet it is nearly useless.
So are many Silicon Valley start-ups.

Asparagus grows explosively, upward of six inches in a 24-hour period. Some farmers harvest it after only a few hours and rarely wait a week. For farmers it is a great crop. Rapid growth leads to a quick profit, though a small one because there are a lot of competing farmers and not all that much demand for asparagus compared with other crops.

Nutritionally, though, asparagus is of limited value. It has only a trace amount of protein, even less fiber, and less than 1 percent of the minimum daily needs for many vitamins. Despite its ability to grow rapidly, a person might starve on a diet of asparagus and probably chase away his or her friends and family because of the perpetual stench it creates when cooked.

In Silicon Valley, companies are farmed like asparagus. Seed companies are overwatered with venture capital money, and so they "grow" quickly and then are harvested by selling them off.

Growth in start-ups is focused on creating "first mover" advantages that appeal to larger companies that don't want to risk innovating in one or another arena. When sold, these start-ups often have very little in terms of real value and the premiums paid for them are like the water you buy prepackaged in asparagus stalks (about 93 percent of its weight).

Growth is what every entrepreneur aspires to. The question then becomes, what kind of growth? There is slow growth through perceived safety in the founder's risk aversion. There is asparagus-like growth, fast but ultimately meaningless. Or there is highly nutritious growth that delivers a cornucopia's worth of dietary value to founders, employees, investors, and the community.

Entrepreneurs often mismanage growth with asparagus farmer mindsets. Sometimes investors lead them toward irrational expansion. Occasionally an entrepreneur missteps and guides his company into rocky fields. Often, inattention to changing market dynamics quickly puts a company at a competitive disadvantage. In all cases the entrepreneur was not closely enough involved with the details of growth planning or was not actively participating in strategic growth initiatives.

The bigger the risk is, the more the entrepreneur needs to be involved.

Early in Micrel's rapid growth of the 1990s we developed a product line for the mobile communications space, which was entering its own hypergrowth phase. Micrel was not incredibly well known at the time, at least in the telecommunications industry. We had not yet established ourselves, and so we wanted to create some breakthrough technology. The question was how.

At that time, the communications protocols from cellular towers to cell phones were evolving. The TDMA (time division multiple access) standard championed by Motorola was favored in the market, but Qualcomm had devised a slick competing protocol that the industry called CDMA (code division multiple access). CDMA had significant technical advantages, but as a newcomer it had no market traction. I made the decision to be part of the CDMA chip market on the basis of an analysis that showed that it would have a significant presence and that there were few competing chip makers in the market. It was an educated gamble.

We got involved with Qualcomm and, with our knowledge of the subject, made products for the power management of CDMA gear. Yet I was worried. Despite a strong partner, a high-growth industry, and the protocol's technical advantages, I was bringing risk to Micrel. If CDMA did not take off as I expected it to, we would have bet on the wrong horse, investing money, labor power, and opportunity costs for naught.

I got personally involved in the project all the way down to design aspects of the chips. I was into the bowels of decision making. Since the risk was high—banking so much of the company on a new technology and market—I had to make sure that what Micrel did was precise. We used an advantageous technology called superbeta that allowed us to make better power management products. We collaborated with phone makers, Qualcomm, and everyone connected to the industry to refine products. We tossed loaded dice.

It did pay off. Even today this one decision, this one product line, is helping us in the mobile industry.

In every company but especially in entrepreneurial start-ups, there is constant friction between maintaining control of the organization and encouraging employees to focus on growth, to take the chances that one must in order to expand. The smaller the company or the larger the risk is, the greater the friction becomes. Company size and the size of a project are both elements of risk, and the greatest dangers come when small companies place large bets. It worked for me and Micrel when we entered the CDMA market, but it hasn't worked so well for other companies.

The key to managing growth, and hence controlling the company, is assuring that everybody is on the same page. People with different missions, agendas, cultures, and product ideas will never achieve rational, much less sustainable growth. Like a platoon of soldiers marching in different directions, they cannot fight the same fight and thus win the battle. Getting growth alignment is the CEO's job, and it involves culture, hiring, communicating, and the CEO's deep involvement.

Hiring the right people, the ones who understand the business, understand the company, and adapt to the culture, is as essential to corporate growth as putting soldiers through the same boot camp is to winning a war. Coordinated discipline in the pursuit of growth cannot be accomplished without a group of similarly enculturated people. Wise, culture-focused hiring prevents divergent missions. When harmony is created between different business units and within the team, growing products and markets becomes part of normal operations (and a CEO can be more hands-off, at least on the less strategic initiatives).

Next, when the company's vision, strategy, and issues are well communicated, employees understand their goals and limits and thus are willing to grow within the framework the CEO specifies. Transparent communications breed trust in following the CEO, which gives employees the permission to pursue growth and, just as important, the trust to slow down when the CEO sees it to be essential. Without that trust, proactive slowing of growth will cause employees to bolt, to either work in confusion or work for someone else.

In this, my thirty-seventh and last year at Micrel's helm, I have seen that whenever employees fully understood and accepted the issues that we faced, they stuck with me. We have had our share of hard times, and a small number of employees bailed. But our retention and rehire rates show that a growth-oriented culture with trusted leadership causes teammates to stay. They rallied around the Micrel vision because they believed we were heading in the right direction for all the right reasons. I have seen other semiconductor companies that did not have the right culture, hired for convenience, and did not communicate their growth plans properly. When they throttled down, their employees did not have the latitude to adjust, became disenchanted, and left.

When does an entrepreneur or even a settled CEO know that growth is not occurring in a sound way? This happens when he is no longer paying attention to the details and mechanics of growth.

We already understand the money hunt that start-up CEOs endure when running on venture capital. As with any large-scale distraction, the time spent raising funds keeps the entrepreneur from sculpting his company, which includes participating in growth-oriented details. This may be the single most challenging problem start-ups face.

Some CEOs, in small and large companies alike, often become high-priced road warriors, busy promoting products and promoting the company, not back home running the show. Unable to escape their desire to be showmen, they delegate the wrong activity, having people not in charge of the mission and vision plan corporate growth, which is all about mission and vision. When I find myself spending more than 25 percent of the time on the road, I make changes so that I can spend at least 75 percent of a year at Micrel guiding expansion.

Being involved also requires not being involved. People do not obtain a sense of value when you control their every action, and this applies especially to creative activities. You can kill people's passion if you direct the way they bring an idea to life. But in that 75 percent of the time an entrepreneur spends at the home office, she needs to get down into the weeds on everything related to growth. Sometimes this involves rolling up her sleeves and participating in the creation of growth, and at other times it requires only watching and monitoring. At either extreme and at all points in between, it does involve the CEO's participation.

Foremost in the CEO's involvement is ensuring alignment. Your team needs the flexibility to execute on the growth plan you have created with them, and you certainly were there during the planning (if you were not, you have more basic problems with which to deal). Employee flexibility in the execution of the plan does not allow you to abdicate your proper level of monitoring and control. Oddly, being too hands-off brings about distrust because employees notice when their leaders are not engaged. They see that you don't understand the complications and roadblocks they face. Your people, if you hired wisely, aren't stupid and will sense noninvolvement and will not follow.

Assuming you have created a growth-oriented culture, have matriculated new candidates properly, and are engaged in the management and monitoring of your growth, external factors can disrupt meaningful expansion. For many companies in Silicon Valley and other tech hubs around the world, this disruption comes from their investors: the venture capitalists who gave them a leg up.

The good and bad news is that venture capitalists participate in the management of their portfolio companies. With the goal of quick profits, VC input into growth is rarely fixated on making sound, stepwise growth decisions. Since 9 in 10 of their investments do not pay off, VCs have a built-in risk margin higher than what entrepreneurs should have in creating an enduring company. Through their participation, VCs will guide their portfolio companies toward anything that exhibits fast, asparagus-type growth. They want to get their harvest of investments to market as fast as they can and are not concerned with the nutritional quality of those crops.

The disquieting effect this has internally is borne by the employees. The entrepreneur started with a vision. He saw products and markets and had a long-term view of how the world might be different and attracted people to help achieve that vision. Saddled with venture capital and less control and probably on the money hunt again, the entrepreneur can be persuaded to chase fast growth that feeds a sell-out exit strategy as opposed to steady growth that feeds people. This ultimate distraction breaks the alignment the entrepreneur creates with the employees, and this is noticed. Without trust, culture-driven growth abates.

But if you don't take care of your investors, you're going to lose your job and the company you kick-started. It's about loyalties to investors, your employees, or your vision.

Unfortunately, most venture capitalists view themselves as being smarter than the companies in which they invest. Despite having never run a business past an early exit, some think they know how to run your business better than you do. These activist investors often show their ignorance of your business in colorful ways.

Circuit City showed how activist investor pressures can cause a company to lose focus on its mission and differentiation can lead to corporate collapse. Circuit City was a stock investor's dream in the 1980s and early 1990s. It entered a market dominated by mom-and-pop retailers, engineered out everything people hated about buying consumer electronics, and grew like a weed. Its growth was based in no small part on having highly trained and commission-incented salespeople who guided customers to buying the right products in an increasingly complex electronics market.

Circuit City's competitive situation changed as Best Buy came to life. Under pressure from many fronts, including certain investors, it abandoned its dedicated sales team and devolved into the Kmart of consumer electronics. Its sales, revenues, and corporate lifeblood evaporated. Instead of understanding the shifting market and knowing how to use its existing differentiation to extend its long-term success, it buckled to short-term profit motives and imploded.

Activist investors simply don't have and are not profoundly interested in having a deep and working knowledge of the company. It doesn't matter if activist shareholders are seeking to artificially boost short-term profits or force a company to serve only fair trade coffee in the cafeteria. Profit or a desire for social change is irrelevant. Those investors' mindset and agenda are not those of the company as a whole: integrated organization in pursuit of a mission, long-term profitability, and equally long-term shareholder returns. Micrel has been public for 20 years, and we have been attacked twice by activists, once in 2008 and again in 2014. The agenda of profit-motivated activists is usually the same: make some changes that they believe will increase the stock price just long enough for them to get out. Unlike regular investors in the public markets who will simply sell your stock if they do not like the direction of the company, activist investors have a very short time horizon and are disruptive to companies by design.

This includes activist VCs. When they "help" you run your company, it can be very bad news. The time for preparation and the time to decide are different phases, and venture capitalists can muddy the distinction. The time for the VCs to prepare is when they evaluate a prospective company. Once that preparation is complete, that's the end of it; they can't prepare anymore. The decision to invest (or not) has been made. Then they have to sit back and take the consequences. Once they attempt to run the company themselves, they have in effect reneged on their decision and are attempting to supplement or replace leadership within the company, creating a multiheaded monster. If they succeed in disrupting a company enough, they can blame the entrepreneurial CEO for a lack of short-term profit even if the CEO has been planning a sound long-term growth strategy. They may decide to pull the CEO and put another in, with the result that the same problems play out through different actors. The new CEO may bring his own guys in, and that will disrupt the organization in new and unique ways.

The real problem is that the venture guys become impatient because of their time constraint and the need to return money to their shareholders. The inherent conflict is between the VC's three-year horizon and the entrepreneur's lifetime one. The former requires any form of rapid growth, the latter a more careful and culturally aligned growth strategy. The two are incompatible, and it is a rare VC who tolerates the long view, who will take the time to learn the people, the environment, and the market dynamics.

In light of the pitfalls of growing too fast, too slow, or with inexpert external guidance, the looming question for an entrepreneur is when and how to ramp up. If you are one of many players with a poorly differentiated offering, it is nearly impossible. Large companies or mass consumer markets are reluctant to give you a break. Stick with it, get a bit bigger, and obtain an established track record and you might open a few doors.

Conversely, you can try to be like everybody else in Silicon Valley by being different from everyone else in Silicon Valley. If you do create groundbreaking, earth-shattering technology that is a game changer, the largest companies suddenly become your best customers. They will take a chance on you because you help them stay ahead of their competition. Even if you are not revolutionary, being first into a market championed by a big player—as when Micrel entered Qualcomm's nascent CDMA telecommunications market—can give you collateral traction. "Big brothers" will invest in you to keep you alive and grow their ecosystems. Size doesn't matter when you have a valuable invention, but it does when your offering isn't unique.

Ramping up—the point in time when you can risk calculated growth—is defined by when you add exceptional value. What you offer has to be unique and valuable on its own or has to contribute to an important industry early. There are very few exceptions to this, and it is worth getting outside assessment about whether you fit in either of the two viable positions.

This applies to even VC-oriented sell-up and sell-out strategies. Unless there is a clear path to finding lift, being either uniquely valuable or being an early entrant into an important ecosystem, the chance of growing enough to be acquired is remote. This is where a lot of risk is wasted in Silicon Valley. When the game is to develop technology and be acquired, the risk comes from nearly instant commoditization of a technology or having your invention be replaced by something newer and better. Some technology has the shelf life of milk, and a lot of venture capital has vanished by backing such products.

After 37 years, Micrel is in the enviable position of picking and choosing acquisition candidates, selecting only those which have created something important and clever and also integrate well into our overall product line. These companies often consist of little more than the founders, the core product, some intellectual property, and a trace of VC money left in the checking account. It doesn't mean their technology is poor but that they did not create it within a company designed to last. They got their sell-out exit, but for a dime on each VC dollar.

Among the companies Micrel has acquired and those which I have watched other companies snag, one common theme appears to be that the acquired company tried to be too big too fast. Their eyes were bigger than their stomachs, and so they initiated product development with multiyear targets that were very costly to develop. By the time they finally got a product to market, the market had changed, the projected margins had shrunk, and they never showed an adequate return to their investors.

Basically, these companies underestimated how long it was going to take them to develop the technology for their products; they tried to ramp up instantly instead of building slowly until the time for bigger risk was right. I tell my engineers that it takes twice as long as they think it will to do anything, whether it is building a house or designing a new chip. It will take twice as long, cost twice the money, and make you pull out twice as much hair from your head. If you plan for that, you may still be able to ramp up big even in your start-up phase, but the risk is still inappropriate.

The catch-22 for entrepreneurs is not going too far in the conservative direction. Zero risk results in zero rewards. If one is too pessimistic in one's risk assessment of engineering build estimates, no investors are less likely to hand over their cash. Even abject realism can dissuade many investors. Putting forth inaccurate yet grandiose plans may excite investors, but you are engineering your own failure.

Aside from external interference and an incomplete growth-oriented culture, spending is the worst growth-limiting habit an entrepreneur can acquire. He can be too tightfisted, stunting growth by not investing appropriately, or he can spend recklessly and drain money from investment-worthy application of cash. It is a balancing act that is not unlike riding a horse. If you are too loose with the reins, a horse will get away from you. Ride too tight and the horse doesn't understand what you want it to do and will more than likely buck you off.

You'll know when you run too tight. Your growth rate will slow substantially, and you'll see your team quitting and moving on because they want a chance to win elsewhere. To have value, they too need success. Their only opportunity to win is if they get products out, preferably exciting products, not mundane or unsexy ones. If you are not investing in markets and products that win consistently, if your risk appetite is low and you don't give your team the cash they need to succeed, they will find someone else to win with.

You have to be careful about how loose you leave the cash reins or how tightly you hold them and be willing to change tension as conditions shift. There's a time to tighten, and there's a time to lighten. When the terrain is rough and uncertain, you need to control your animal and your company closely. But when you come to a flat meadow, letting horses and employees gallop gets you to your goal faster. You loosen the reins when a group is working well and achieving sound growth: advancing into a market segment or inventing a new product. You tighten the reins when you find your organization stumbling, when markets are not going in the direction that was originally forecast.

Nobody enjoys tightening the reins, but it rarely kills a business, at least in the short term. It is almost impossible to be too tightfisted, and if you are, your employees will let you know by pushing back or packing up. Usually it is the other way around. Many more companies fail because they run too loose, making multiple advances simultaneously or placing insanely large bets on one market or product. Enabled by venture partners, more than a few thousand firms spend cash like there's no tomorrow, as if they have to throw it all in to win today.

If you have limited resources, you have no choice but to run your company tightly or you will go out of business. By the same token, if you don't have the discipline to meter those funds, you risk running out of money because you will spend it too quickly. One risk of cash depletion comes from moving faster than you are able to control. Remember the first time you thundered down a steep hill on your bicycle and crashed? You were moving faster than your youthful capabilities allowed. In business, the faster you move, the more mistakes you make per unit of time. The same number of mistakes spread out over longer periods allows for graceful adjustments, but compressed into venture capital ROI time frames, that set of mistakes can be fatal.

A critical growth decision each entrepreneur must eventually make is whether to grow vertically or horizontally. Both work, but how well they work depends on the specific markets, the competitive pressures, and the core competency in your company. Vertical market penetration—trying to assemble all the pieces in a whole product—usually takes more investment because you have to penetrate deeply into the market you want to serve. It also carries substantially more risk because if the market goes through a disruptive change, such as those the personal computing market is now enduring, your investment and work can become unprofitable. Vertical integration also carries a timewise product-readiness risk: if you don't hit the milestones that you promised, you will not make your numbers and your company will probably be sold off.

Horizontal markets can be approached with less risk but require deeper channel knowledge and capabilities. You are part of an ecosystem and thus sell through partners who spread your product. It is less risky than vertical products because you do less expensive and faster development, but your market penetration and growth will be slower. It will take time to develop a broad product portfolio in horizontal markets or across multiple markets.

For many entrepreneurs, the end goal, the grand mission, is to become both: to be an integrated company. In the semiconductor industry, there are a few heavyweights that have a broad portfolio of point solutions as well as integrated solution sets. None of these companies started life that way. These big players have deep pockets, which is necessary to sustain the development expense as well as buffer the risks they face in simultaneously moving horizontally and vertically.

If you plan on selling out, a big gamble on a vertical market approach is not insane, but it is risky. If instead you want to build an enduring company, one your great-grandchildren will talk about, horizontal companies tend to be more successful because they are able to survive by not being a one-trick pony. Horizontally focused firms have many irons in the fire and grow through numerous small steps instead of a single giant leap. These are the companies venture capitalists dislike because a safer and saner growth strategy is too sluggish for their taste.

The other growth strategy comes from mergers and acquisitions (M&As). Aside from start-ups planning to be acquired, M&A is a growth mechanism that applies mainly to established companies, though small firms and even start-ups have been known to merge.

M&As happen for a lot of reasons. Generally, mergers occur between two relatively equal companies. In Silicon Valley the classic example was when Hewlett-Packard merged with Compaq. Unlike mergers, acquisitions occur mainly because the smaller company has a key technology that a larger company wants. The motivations for buying a company instead of building a competing product are varied, with patents, time to market, and competitive pressures being the most common.

In both cases, an M&A's value lies in completing a company's market mission. Hewlett-Packard was already in the personal computer business before it considered merging with Compaq. But Compaq had highly refined manufacturing processes and made computers more affordably and with higher margins than its competitors, and that was important in a rapidly commoditizing market. At that time Hewlett-Packard customers had started using personal computing technologies for office servers, and that trend showed no signs of slowing (today most servers around the globe are basically hyped-up personal computers). Hewlett-Packard was merging in order to have efficient manufacturing operations that would create better profitability in two major product areas: PCs and servers. Compaq provided a defined value, namely, efficiency.

Acquisitions are done for the same reason, though time to market and blocking competitors drive most acquisition decisions in Silicon Valley. Almost daily we hear of some tiny company with hardly any track record being acquired for many multiples of its assumed valuation, and some of those valuations are purely fictional. These are the 1-in-10 payoffs for venture capitalists. Most commonly, a key technology developed by the acquired company provides larger companies with a field-tested approach to a specific value add to their existing product line that competitors are also eager to have. When this is covered by intellectual property, a timely acquisition is valuable both as a revenue or market share accelerator and as a competitive blocking maneuver.

Regardless of the mode—merger or acquisition—or the justification for M&As, the endgame derives from presumed synergies between the two companies that allegedly allow them to grow faster than they were able to individually. The growth can be top line, as some companies have done, adding more and more revenue producers to the portfolio. At times this is rational, as when the merged products are complementary. Sometimes it is nonsensical, as when Cisco bought a personal video recorder company that had nothing to do with its core business in networking gear. Other times the synergy delivers bottom-line results, such as when Hewlett-Packard received operational efficiencies in building personal computers. Often it comes from market consolidation, which hampers competitors by creating market dominance and scale.

Of these three major rationales for M&As, acquiring strictly for revenue is not always a good strategy. Sometimes the market or investors push CEOs to acquire companies just for top-line revenue, but that alone isn't wise. There has to be a fit. Imagine a successful track runner, a sprinter. He has won championships by running swiftly on his two legs. If he was advised to surgically add a wheel to his body, odds are that it would result in his not being able to run at all. It isn't a fit. Cisco buying a flip camcorder company was not a fit either.

One reason these ill-fitting top-line growth acquisitions are a mistake comes from integrating the acquired company. A corporation has a mission and has developed a culture, policies, procedures, and internal operations to achieve that mission. Any acquired company will have to be integrated into the existing firm. This requires time, and the more different the acquired company is, the more time it will take. Several Silicon Valley semiconductor companies nearly failed during acquisition sprees because they could not integrate even similar companies with compatible product lines rapidly enough.

Micrel's benchmark for acquisitions is that an acquired company must be integrated within a year and a half. If it cannot, it is probably a poor fit within Micrel's mission and product portfolio. It means the synergies aren't there and the capital and employee effort to integrate the acquired company would be better invested in internal growth. Slow integration affects revenue and thus ROI. If you cannot achieve targeted ROI in less than two years, it is a poor investment compared with the alternatives.

That's the first requirement to justify an acquisition. The others include the following:

- Within the same year and a half, we need to see gross margins of 50 percent from the target company's products. Gross margin must be in the range of 40 percent or higher for us even to consider the acquisition.

- The acquisition has to be in markets that Micrel currently serves so that it does not dilute engineering or sales resources.
- If it's a technology-driven acquisition, the technology has to be unique and in a market that's growing rapidly.
- We prefer, although it is not mandatory, to have the target company in the San Francisco Bay Area to smooth the transition.
- The acquisition cannot take Micrel's earnings negative during the year and a half after acquisition.
- The target company's revenue growth rate has to be equal to or greater than Micrel's.
- The acquisition cannot require Micrel to take on significant debt.
- Last but not least, there must be a culture fit between the two companies.

The common mode of acquisitions in Silicon Valley is similar to gutting fish. Generally, the acquiring firm gets rid of everybody in the acquired company, keeping only the intellectual property, key staff to help with the transition, and occasionally above-average engineering talent. Often the acquired company has traction, and so it becomes a mere cash cow for the acquiring company. From a financial point of view that's not a bad business model, but from an integrity perspective it is unreasonable. Such "acquire and fire" plans ruin a lot of people's lives, exposing dedicated employees and their families to unemployment just to make a few bucks. You have to be a bit heartless to do such acquisitions routinely.

Some industries go through M&A spasms in which acquiring companies simply go nuts. My own semiconductor industry is one that does this on a regular basis as competitive pressures drive market consolidation. As more competitors enter any market, competitive costs rise while prices and margins fall. Eventually, smaller companies suffer and become ripe for harvesting. All too often activist investors force a CEO's hand and drive acquisition campaigns in the belief that there ought to be consolidation. That's a joke. The only reason an investor should want consolidation is that on one side there's going to be a premium and it wants the stock to rise, not to defy normal market mechanics.

If you are a regular shareholder or a shareholding employee, this is bad news. Such acquisition campaigns can cause short-term surges in the share price of the acquiring company, and that is when the activist investors sell their shares—a harsh form of pump and dump. But if you are a normal buy-and-hold investor or an employee with stock options, you soon discover that the share price surge is temporary and that the acquiring company's stock rapidly falls because of the cost/profit lag during the integration period.

Merger and acquisition insanity comes from the desire for growth without measuring the long-term impacts. Short-term results are possible. In a few months or a year, the assumed synergistic effect—real or imagined—can motivate employees and excite the stock market. But the long-term effects—the time to integrate acquisitions, the lost opportunity costs, the dilution of culture and brand in a merger—have deep implications. Zeal to drive top-line revenue can destroy bottom-line results, though the latter appears a while after the former. M&A for the sake of revenue is a dumb idea.

This is where even experienced CEOs can fall victim to M&A insanity. It is an early sign of doom when shareholders or the investment community tells a CEO how to do business, informing her that she must drive top-line revenues higher and higher. The pressure to achieve revenues above profits cheats the very notion of running a business. Activist shareholders have tried to get incompatible media and content companies to merge, which might have generated more short-term top-line revenues. But in most of these cases the companies, their histories, their markets, and their cultures would be a tough fit and completely integrating them would take a long time. The long term, however, isn't what those activist shareholders wanted, seeking instead a premium on that stock. Microsoft at one time toyed with buying Yahoo, which would have been an even tougher fit. Luckily for Microsoft, Yahoo didn't want to join despite the significant premium its shareholders would have received. Sometimes a CEO is forced to capitulate when activist shareholders have the leverage to take over the company and thus do whatever they want. But as a servant leader, he more typically educates the nonactivist shareholders, explaining the long-term goals and associated returns.

When competing forces are evaluated—cost, complexity, product and culture fit, competitive pressures, stockholder returns—proper mergers and acquisitions should occur only when it is best for both companies. Whether you are being merged or are going to be acquired or if you are acquiring somebody else, make sure the deal works for everyone. When it doesn't, you create more resistance to change and the end result will always disappoint.

When young entrepreneurs ask me about growing their companies, I ask them how they intend to grow as people. If they are building an enduring business, they are taking the long view and making a lifetime commitment. Thus, any move toward growth needs to match the entrepreneur's life plan. If it suits his needs, the needs of his employees, and the needs of his company, the right and wrong growth strategies typically become obvious. When an entrepreneur is committed to his or her company for life, rash and risky growth gimmicks also become obvious, as do the motivations of activist investors. The true entrepreneur, the man or woman with the passion, discipline, and confidence to achieve a vision will grow and will do so on his or her own schedule.

LESSONS

* Growth is what every entrepreneur aspires to. The question then becomes, what kind of growth?
* The bigger the risk is, the more the entrepreneur needs to be involved.
* There is constant friction between maintaining control of the organization and encouraging employees to focus on growth. The key to managing growth is assuring that everybody is on the same page.
* Being involved also requires not being involved. People do not obtain a sense of value when you control their every action. Yet being too hands-off brings about distrust: employees notice when their leaders are not engaged.
* With their goal of quick profits, VCs' input into growth is rarely fixated on making sound, stepwise growth decisions. The disquieting effect this has internally is on your employees.
* Activist investors simply don't have and are not profoundly interested in having a deep and working knowledge of the company. Their universal agenda is to make some changes they believe will increase the stock price just long enough for them to get out.
* Ramping up—the point in time when you can risk calculated growth—is defined by when you add exceptional value.
* The common mode of acquisitions in Silicon Valley is similar to gutting fish: the acquiring firm gets rid of everybody in the acquired company, keeping only the intellectual property and key staff to help with the transition.

Developing Your Plan for Entrepreneurial Success

I f it were easy, anyone could do it.

You are not just anyone. That you have this book in your hands proves you are not the average wage earner. You are an entrepreneur or an aggressive manager who wants to create and lead an enterprise with a purpose; you have a vision and are excited about the journey. The fact is that it isn't easy; the path to your objectives is strewn with difficult and seemingly unappetizing tasks, but since none of this is deterring you, you are an entrepreneur. You crave challenge and love learning by doing. Your vision, passion, and plan for your life are pushing you toward leadership.

All you need is the discipline to achieve it.

It won't be easy. Nothing worth obtaining ever is. Problems will appear to be huge. People with other agendas will obstruct your path. Revenues will always seem too low and expenses too high. Some days it will appear to be one struggle after another. Yet strength and struggle go together. To only "try" is weak. To do "the best I can" is not strong enough. You must always do better than you think you can.

Without discipline, nothing much happens. Life goes on, but in the mediocrity of mere survival. We humans flourished because our brains allowed us to see better ways, and with those visions of a better life, we developed the disciplines necessary to inch forward. The first humanoid who tried to tame fire probably didn't survive the experience, but others learned from his mistakes and harnessed the fundamental tools of the Bronze Age. Benjamin Franklin experimented with electricity and kept church steeples from being scorched by lightning, but his driven tinkering was the first step toward a computer and information society. In each case the vision of something better instilled the discipline to try, try, try.

Discipline above all else is the mark of an entrepreneur. Business objectives are abstract, and the means for creating a business are detailed. The entrepreneur connects thousands of boring details together through the discipline of doing tough things first. He may have a grand vision of a product line but must first gather some start-up capital. He may see how to navigate his industry to achieve a position of dominance but starts by crafting a culture that can execute that goal. He wants to see money roll in and fund expansion but first learns industry metrics and formulates cash management plans to ensure growth. He rolls up each sleeve and tackles a thousand things he has little interest in aside from the interest in creating an organization that feeds itself, grows itself, and exceeds its own expectations.

The entrepreneur does the tough things first. One of the toughest things is getting started and seeing how to make the mission happen. To get there, you need four basic elements.

START

Jim Fixx was a friend of mine. He was a runner and a passionate one. He popularized running as a personal sport and is largely responsible for all the people you see jogging down the road before and after work. We became friends when I developed a gizmo called the Microcell Racer, a marathoner's watch that predated all the modern wearable fitness devices. Jim owned one, and we chatted about our various athletic histories. He mentioned me and the Microcell Racer in his *Second Book of Running*.

Jim died of a heart attack, not from running but from massively clogged arteries in his congenitally enlarged heart. Recently another friend of mine went down to the beach but never made it out of his truck. We all will die someday, and the only regret worth having is to have never tried while breathing.

Becoming an entrepreneur, launching a business, setting your life around this one endeavor, is daunting. Fear keeps many people from trying. That may be the single biggest hurdle, the toughest thing you must first do. It is a risk and often a leap of faith. Yet if you have the drive, know how to solve problems, and develop the discipline to do tough things first, risk fades and the thrill of architecting a lasting enterprise becomes your enduring passion.

But you must start. Everything else is meaningless until you do.

The Entrepreneur's Plan for His or Her Company

There are seven essential aspects to planning a company. These are tough things to do first and to redo as needed.

- **A financial operations model:** Make a commitment up front to the various milestones that you want to achieve. These milestones should be realistic but firm. Do not deviate from your plans unless something catastrophic happens. Run your operations to that plan. This is called *modeling* your company. You need to build two different kinds of models: a model to show investors and a model that you actually use to run the company, with the latter being more aggressive and hence more profitable than the former. Having two models is not dishonest because investors' expectations and your goals are different things. As long as you deliver on both models, everybody is happy that his or her goals have been met.

- **An exit strategy:** I am hijacking an in vogue term that serial entrepreneurs use, but the idea is similar. You need an end goal. That goal may be to run your enterprise until old age leaves you unable to get to the office anymore, or it could be to sell your company to Google in three years. It may be to IPO your company within five years, or you can take the SAS route and stay private while generating billions in revenues. Without an exit strategy, you have no business plan. Telling yourself, "We'll just see how it goes," doesn't work, and no investor will give you a dime. Make this decision before you are forced to make a decision under duress.

- **Principles:** Having and communicating a set of principles— your ethical guidelines and policies that you establish up front— allows you to make decisions in advance and delegate those predecisions to everybody in the company. Principle-based policies are successful decisions made in advance because the implications have already been considered and everybody in the company knows what choices to make. Make the decision or have a decision-making model before you have to decide.

- **Backup plans:** What is a safety net? Something will go wrong eventually. Most of the time it is small; other times it is catastrophic. I have endured five different business cycles and have had three different customers, each providing over 20 percent of Micrel's revenue, pull the plug. In all these instances we had alternatives, fallback strategies for how we would continue. You need two or three options to execute when your original plan and goals are changed. Two or more backup plans are necessary because by the time you need to execute a backup, it may not be appropriate and you will need to fall back again.

- **Good mental health:** You are the mind of your organization, and a diseased mind produces unpredictable results. Keeping calm, keeping your wits, and keeping your body in shape and your mind proactive allow you to execute your plan with the focus necessary over the long term. Since adversity is going to visit your business, stay mentally healthy by recognizing this as a challenge, a puzzle to solve. Calmly dealing with catastrophe, tragedies, and emergencies is part of running a mentally healthy business. Having good mental health in the office begins with having a good family life, and having good physical health is essential. Abandoning any tendency toward a woe-is-me attitude is a requirement, for complaining motivates nobody.

- **Resiliency:** Enduring businesses are marathons, not sprints. You must have tremendous staying power and be able to run on empty. Runners talk about hitting the wall, a point in an endurance race where the mind and body conspire to collapse.

Your legs lock up, and you feel you cannot take another step. But all marathon runners have encountered this, and they push through the torment. They keep moving. They may run more slowly, or they may even just walk. But they don't stop. A CEO friend of mine was running a marathon, and his legs seized up on him. He thought that he was not going to be able to finish the race. He quite literally could not move his legs because of how badly they were cramping. He said a prayer and asked God to help him, and wouldn't you know, he started moving again. "I just never gave up; I started moving forward. The cramps relieved themselves, and I was able to continue with the race." Be resilient and never be afraid to say a little prayer. There is nothing wrong with getting on your knees and asking God for help.

Humility: Management is about getting things done through people, and when all is finally laid to rest, we are all very similar. We have emotions, we have dreams, we prefer kindness, and we want to help one another. An entrepreneur needs to be in a humble state of mind to accept help and to give it effectively. She must listen more than she talks, and she must serve her employees so that they can be more fulfilled and lead better lives. Being prideful accomplishes little. Being arrogant and egotistical destroys. Being humble, aside from being proper, also motivates others to want to help you, and that means helping you succeed in building your business.

PERSONAL DISCIPLINE AND YOUR PLAN

There is no such thing as nonpersonal discipline. Discipline may exist organizationwide, but that is the collective individual discipline of all the employees.

Since you lead the organization, your self-discipline is every-thing, and discipline is doing what you don't like doing and doing it well.

Great entrepreneurs develop great personal discipline. Numer-ous books about the titans of industry all show that they were highly disciplined people. They set priorities, mapped objectives, and paid attention to a million things that most people might find tedious, demanding, and uninteresting. Yet that is why they succeeded. Their discipline came before success and continued throughout. It was very personal. In a world where people crave leisure, look for short-cuts, and do not expect great quality, entrepreneurs who discipline themselves to do the tough things first change things in big ways.

This discipline of doing tough things first is part of the marathon of creating an enduring business. Thousands of issues will not be completed soon and will be replaced with a thousand different issues as the company grows. The discipline of working through business issues is a commitment to your entrepreneurial plan and your life plan. After all, what kind of plan is it if you're not committed? Dis-pel any notion you may have that running a company is going to be perpetually wonderful, easy, and rosy. That's like believing that run-ning a marathon is no different from walking to the corner store on a warm spring afternoon. It's an endurance race. Only tenacious and vigilant entrepreneurs will finish it.

Communicating Your Vision and Project

Your primary job as a CEO is to plan and communicate, with the lat-ter being vastly important and a skill that few people natively pos-sess. As wonderful as giving speeches and pontificating may be, when it comes to leading your employees, listening is the form of communication you will learn to rely on.

Learning to listen, to ask questions, to clarify in an almost Socratic mode does two things: it helps employees think through problems and by doing so makes them fully enfranchised members of the company. It increases the personal self-perception of the employees while they explore and establish the best solutions. It helps employees grow as people, which increases their value. I tell my employees that I may not be able to make them rich, but I will do everything I can to make them better people.

When Micrel had its only unprofitable year, we needed to consolidate our fabrication facilities. There simply wasn't enough business in our refocused product lines to justify having two plants. This wasn't an absolute certainty, but it was very likely. Our CFO suggested doing it early on, but I didn't approve of the project. He was, in a word, confused. He came back a few more times, and I kept saying, "You don't get it," prodding him to reevaluate his approach to the problem. Months and many discussions later he had a gleam in his eye as he announced that we should wait a little longer because even though the need to consolidate was likely, there was not yet an indisputable need to do so.

He got it. I could have explained that to him much earlier, but that would have been autocratic command-and-control management. I preferred to have him think through all the implications of consolidating our fabrication facilities, examine the write-off we would take, and see how that would create our first unprofitable year on paper. He finally understood that waiting until the need was undeniable would give us the flexibility to maintain our unbroken winning streak should consolidation be unnecessary. It was better for him to reach a conclusion that I already had, because now he owned the outcome.

The Entrepreneur's Life

Accept that entrepreneurialism is your life, not just a piece of it.

Much has been said about finding a work/life balance and compartmentalizing the two. This is a luxury that entrepreneurs do not have. Give up on the notion that you have life at work and life at home. They will be integrated. When you have business plans in a constant state of review in your mind, when you have hundreds or thousands of employees to whom you are a servant leader, when their futures are dependent on your making payroll, your workday never really stops. Trying to separate work and home is impossible.

This does not mean your personal life becomes all-encompassing work. Doing this would destroy you as a whole person. Entrepreneurs learn to incorporate their work with their personal lives. Instead of rigidly compartmentalizing work and nonwork time, entrepreneurs learn to prioritize and put each element of their lives in perspective.

For entrepreneurs, life is their passion and work is part of life. Thus, your work is part of your life passion. So is providing for your family, participating in sports, giving to your community, and managing your business. You learn that each of these is a challenge, a joy, and part of your personal fulfilment. Your business should not be your life, but it is part of your life, incorporated throughout the day as much as breathing and eating. By keeping business in perspective with all other things but not segregating it as a laborious necessity, you find balance while remaining fully involved.

Don't Compromise

This is your life. Your business. Your vision. Your dream. Make sure you live it on your terms.

INDEX

ABOUT THE AUTHOR

Cowboy, gymnast, "vertically challenged" hurdle track star, inventor of industry-wide chip manufacturing inventions, the founder and former CEO of Micrel Corporation, Ray Zinn's approach to life and business led to fundamental evolutions in microchip technology that shrank mainframe computers into smart phones. He went against Silicon Valley's addiction to venture capital and built an international microchip enterprise without outside investors. He suddenly became legally blind mere days before his company was to go public, yet he remained Micrel's leader for another two decades.

Zinn is the founder, and for 37 years was the CEO of Micrel (NASDAQ: MCRL). He founded the Silicon Valley microchip design and manufacturing company in 1978. Micrel is one of the few integrated (design, manufacturing, and testing) chip companies, and one of the very few that keeps its fabrication operations in the United States.

Zinn was born into a ranching family in California's Imperial Valley—the desert region bordering Mexico. Before college he honed his determination, becoming a competitive gymnast and a regional high hurdle competitor despite being—as he puts it— "vertically challenged."

Zinn is credited with conceptualizing the wafer stepper, and selling it to Texas Instruments before it had even been designed.

Forward-looking at its time, the wafer stepper is now a standard piece of equipment in every chip manufacturing facility around the globe.

In 2015, Zinn exited Micrel after 37 years at the helm. With a wealth of precise executive and entrepreneurial wisdom, he is innovating once again, founding Mentor Capital, an entrepreneur accelerator, to help business visionaries build profitable, enduring companies and to change the leadership foundations of Silicon Valley and technology hubs around the globe. With venture capital becoming more restrictive and difficult to obtain, new entrepreneurs will need Mentor Capital's hands-on mentoring as well as funding in order to thrive. By running their companies using lessons presented in *Tough Things First*, Mentor Capital entrepreneurial candidates are assured, as Zinn says, "that we will not let them fail."

CPSIA information can be obtained
at www.ICGtesting.com
Printed in the USA
LVHW02*1737291117
557975LV00005B/7/P